Blessed Life

Blessed Life

My Surprising Journey of Joy, Tears,
and Tales from Harlem to Hollywood

Kim Fields
with Todd Gold

New York Nashville

FaithWords
Hachette Book Group
1290 Avenue of the Americas, New York, NY 10104
faithwords.com
twitter.com/faithwords

First Edition: November 2017

FaithWords is a division of Hachette Book Group, Inc. The FaithWords name and logo are trademarks of Hachette Book Group, Inc.

The publisher is not responsible for websites (or their content) that are not owned by the publisher.

The Hachette Speakers Bureau provides a wide range of authors for speaking events. To find out more, go to www.hachettespeakersbureau.com or call (866) 376-6591.

All photos, unless otherwise indicated, are from the author's personal collection.

The Holy Bible, New International Version®, NIV® Copyright © 1973, 1978, 1984, 2011 by Biblica, Inc.® Used by permission. All rights reserved worldwide.

LCCN: 2017948549

ISBNs: 978-1-4789-4754-7 (hardcover), 978-1-5460-2711-9 (signed), 978-1-5460-2710-2 (B&N signed), 978-1-4789-4755-4 (ebook)

Printed in the United States of America

LSC-C

10 9 8 7 6 5 4 3 2 1

DEDICATION

This book is dedicated to my mother, Chip. Mommy, without you, I would have no life ... let alone a blessed life. Your guidance, grace, prayer, covering, wisdom, discipline, humor, tears, kisses, and hugs set the most amazing foundation for quite a journey we had no idea would be ours ... mine. With the deepest gratitude and love a child can possess for her mother, I give thanks and love to you and to Him for gifting me with you.

kimmy

INSPIRATION

This book was inspired by my husband, Christopher L. Morgan, who for years encouraged me to tell my story. Honey, you continue to amaze me with your love. I'm so very blessed to be your wife and be on this part of the journey of climbing and building with you. I will never forget how you reached far into my soul with "You can't worry and remember at the same time." You are a glorious balm.

All my love & laughs always,

j.

MOTIVATION

This book is motivated by my children, my sons. Firstborn Prince: Sebastian Alexander Morgan and Youngest Prince: Quincy Xavier Morgan. Knowing your history, who you are and what you come from, is a great blessing. I pray this book blesses you not only with life lessons, but with your personal history, your blueprint of the foundation our family—you—is set upon. You both motivate me to be my best Me every day, yet love me dearly through all the times I'm not. I adore you both with all my heart and soul, cherishing your love, laughter, hugs, and kisses all the days of your long/safe/prosperous lives.

STANDING OVATION

Aunt Pat, there aren't enough words nor enough languages for me to express my love and gratitude to you for all the sacrifices you have made and continue to make for me in the name of love. My Lord, how blessed I am and my life is because of you.

ELEVATION

And Alexis...Lex, you are so amazing to my whole soul. Your birth and existence elevated my game as a sister, a friend, and as a person. Your vibe is consistently at the top of my #goals list. I love and adore you.

Well, son, I'll tell you:
Life for me ain't been no crystal stair.

Langston Hughes, "Mother to Son"

Contents

Contents

Talking to Myself

1. The thing that makes me happiest is <u>my family.</u>
2. I always laugh when <u>I think of Robert Downey Jr. in Tropic Thunder.</u>
3. When I'm late, it's usually because <u>of wardrobe changes.</u>
4. I can be annoying when <u>I'm never annoying. (Can you see the winking emoji here?)</u>
5. The thing that bothers me most is <u>bad driving and a lack of manners.</u>
6. My favorite part of being a kid was <u>watching superhero TV shows and swimming.</u>
7. I am always puzzled when people <u>seem entitled.</u>
8. I love <u>the Lord.</u>
9. Right now, at this very minute, I'm feeling <u>motivated. I'm on a spiritual and caffeine groove!</u>
10. In the kitchen, I am <u>basic. . My husband is the chef.</u>
11. As a black woman, I am <u>amazing because He created me regardless of race or gender.</u>
12. When I'm in the shower, I sing <u>Bruno . Mars and Hamilton songs.</u>

13. If I could meet anyone, living or dead, it would be <u>Gregory Hines.</u>

14. And I would ask him, <u>Why'd you leave before we could work and dance together?</u>

15. The thing about men is <u>they are an amazing part of humanity.</u>

16. My favorite movies are <u>most of the classics, , Mary Poppins, Tropic Thunder, , Moulin Rouge!, and Coming to America.</u>

17. The last time I said "I should've," I <u>should've confirmed that the coffee was decaf.</u>

18. The thing I like most in another person is <u>kindness and creativity.</u>

19. If I'm in the grocery store, I can't resist <u>Pepperidge Farm Milano cookies.</u>

20. Nobody knows this about me, but <u>I'm terribly clumsy.</u>

21. My guilty pleasure is <u>Oreo cookie ice cream.</u>

22. I believe in God because <u>His resume with me alone is off the chain, let alone the works of His hand.</u>

23. As the mother of two boys, <u>I stay prayed up.</u>

24. I get scared when <u>I try snow skiing.</u>

25. I wish I was better at <u>snow skiing.</u>

26. The last time I cried, it was because <u>I didn't book a part that I really wanted.</u>

27. My biggest mistake was <u>wearing a thong while horseback riding for 8.5 hours.</u>

28. My favorite part of my body is <u>my legs.</u>

29. In my free time I <u>read.</u>

30. People ordinarily think I'm <u>outgoing.</u>

31. But I'm really <u>shy.</u>

32. My hero is <u>King David.</u>

33. The thing I still want to know is <u>why eggnog isn't a year-round treat.</u>

34. My least favorite thing about myself is my lack of <u>consistency when it comes to working out.</u>

35. I wish I could <u>breathe underwater like Aquaman — and dance all day long.</u>

36. When I go to church on Sunday, I <u>get my praise O.N and love to go deeper in His word.</u>

37. If you want to hang out, I'm apt to say, <u>"Let's see a movie."</u>

38. You'll never catch me without <u>sunglasses.</u>

39. I'm having a good day when <u>my family has what they need and I get to dance.</u>

40. Real faith for me means <u>total surrender to His plan and patiently yet expectantly watching it unfold.</u>

41. If I could play only one song forever, it would be <u>". My Shot" from Hamilton.</u>

42. When I'm stressed, I <u>play some .Maxwell or Fred Hammond — and pause to breathe.</u>

43. My bucket list still includes <u>performing on Broadway and having a waterfront she-shed.</u>

44. When I lay my head on my pillow at night, I <u>read political thrillers to shut off my brain.</u>

45. When all is said and done, I <u>work hard, play hard, love hard, and praise hard.</u>

Introduction

This is my fortieth year in show business. It is my forty-eighth year on this planet.

Milestones are a funny thing. I believe we celebrate them because God has given us the gift of life. I also celebrate them as reminders of all of the amazing gifts in my life. Some of those gifts: I played Tootie on *The Facts of Life*. I was Regine on *Living Single*. I've been on *The Real Housewives of Atlanta* and *Dancing with the Stars*. I am an actor, director, producer, and poet. I am Chip's daughter. I am a sister. I am Christopher Morgan's wife. I am the mother of our two wonderful African American boys, Sebastian and Quincy. I am a friend to many. I am a person of faith.

The list goes on and on. And though I am in a different place than I imagined at this stage of my life—hey, who isn't—more often than not, when I am able to catch my breath between driving in school carpools, reading scripts, and helping with homework, when I turn off *PJ Masks* and *Teen Titans Go!* and curl up next to my husband to catch up on *House of Cards* or *Black Dynamite*, I know that I am right where I should be. Still, too often I find myself, as many of us do, stuck in forward motion. Got to get to the next appointment. Where is the next gig? What's for dinner? What am I going to wear tomorrow? What are the kids going to do for camp next summer? Too often it is about what is next, what I don't have, what I want more of. Instead, I know I need to hit the pause button, appreciate all the amazingness I've been through, and say, "God, look at all you've done for me. Thank you."

This book is the result of me hitting the pause button. I wanted to—and as I discovered, I also needed to—sift through memories and reflect on my journey thus far. Like a lot of people, I'm a working parent, hitting a midlife stride, and facing an uncertain future. I want to be hopeful, but I also have concerns and worries. So I stopped and took stock of where I've been, what's happened to me, and how I've gotten to this place in my life. I saw how I've learned from mistakes and grown from challenges. During the process of looking back, I was reminded of the classic "footprints in the sand" poem, about the man who, as he replays scenes from his life, sees two sets of footprints in the sand, one his and one the Lord's. However, during the lowest periods of his life, he sees only one set of footprints, causing him to question the Lord. He says, "I don't understand why, when I needed You the most, You would leave me." To which the Lord replies, "My precious child, I love you and will never leave you . . . When you saw only one set of footprints, it was then that I carried you."

Armed with the intelligence and wisdom I acquired from going through the past, I emerge hopeful and expectant, feeling like I'm ready for the next phase of my journey. The angels He put on my path to cover me, grow me, challenge me, and protect me were not going to suddenly leave me, and that gave me the ability to look ahead with courage and anticipation (and to be very honest, anxiety at times—should I put "conquer anxiety" on my never-ending to-do list?). That's what I want to pass on to everyone who reads this. Hope, strength, light, memories, and some laughs. Writing this book let me see the remarkable journey I've been on, but it also allowed me to see that we all have, in a sense, been on it together. Though the details may be different, I sense that we may share many similarities. And so this book is for us, both to remind and encourage us that what God had done in our pasts, He will do in our futures.

I hope you read this and are awakened to the many wonderful blessings He has brought forth in your life!

Now, let's start this part of our journey together.

Blessed Life

My Mother's Voice

1

My Mother's Daughter

Everyone has a place they call home. Mine is the area between 136th and 145th Streets and St. Nicholas Avenue in
Harlem. This is where I was born and raised until I was six years
old, and though we moved west, my heart and soul have always
remained in this bosom of black life and culture. I can still see
the red and brown and green brick buildings rising from the
sidewalks and feel the bustle in front of the shops and restaurants. My soul contains the poetry of Langston Hughes, the
stretched-out notes of Duke Ellington, the fist-pounding of
Malcolm X, the inspirations of Ossie Davis and Ruby Dee, and
the singing in St. Phillips Church on Sundays. No matter where
I am, I have the ability to reach out to all those things and feel
replenished from the top of my head to the tips of my toes.
Harlem is where my heart is.

I would not trade growing up in Hollywood, but I love being
able to say I am from Harlem. It conjures up a whole history,
a people, and a culture. Washington, DC, may be the capital of

the United States, but I believe Harlem is this country's soul. This parcel of Manhattan has a distinctive rhythm like no other, and a sound, especially when I say it out loud:

I am from Harlem.

I am from Harlem.

I am. From Harlem.

My maternal grandmother came from a large family in Virginia. I am not sure of their roots beyond that or the roots on the rest of my family's expansive tree. Only recently, while searching the Internet for photos of my friend, actor Tommy Ford, who passed away unexpectedly, did I come across a picture of my mother, Laverne "Chip" Fields, from the touring company of *Hello, Dolly!* in 1975.

I had never seen that particular photo before and wondered where it came from. I clicked on it and up popped a website devoted to all things *Hello, Dolly!* It included a biography of my mom, filled with colorful details about her audition for the show's star, Pearl Bailey, plus bits and pieces of family history that I had never heard before. My mother, it turned out, was born in New York, raised in Virgina by her Aunt Alice and beloved Uncle Louis, then moved back to NYC when she was eight years old to live with her mother (my grandmother), a dancer who went by the name Patsy Styles—something else I did not know until then.

My mom was accepted into New York's prestigious High School of Performing Arts (informally known as PA), later the inspiration for the beloved movie *Fame*. Midway through school, she met Evander High School star basketball player Tony Fields at Harlem's YMCA. The two became high school sweethearts. She got pregnant just before graduation from PA and switched to Newark Prep to get her diploma. Still, she has always joked that I attended the PA, too.

In turn, I have always pictured her as this young woman with a big belly and then a newborn, still driven to perform, determined to learn and practice and perfect her craft. Despite getting pregnant and having a baby at eighteen years of age, she did not drop out or give up. She did not become a statistic. She remained in school, got her diploma, and kept her dream alive.

When I think back on how I kept my focus in the tough moments in my life, I know the source of my grit. I had a role model.

Thanks, Mom.

She and her then-high-school-sweetheart, Tony Fields, married and stayed together for the next five years. I never had a relationship with my dad. I am not throwing shade at him. He is a good man, and when I was around five or six years old, he and mom divorced, and he eventually remarried and had children. I never wondered why he was able to make that situation work and not ours. Timing, maturity, fate—I understood all that and so never had any issues with him not being a father to me. Plus, my village was solid.

We couldn't afford a sitter, so there were times when Mom took me to acting class with her. There were other kids there (whose parents couldn't afford sitters either). To entertain ourselves, we imitated what we saw our parents do. Soon, the Fanns started classes for kids and called us the Mini Ensemble. Danielle Spencer, who would later go on to star as Dee on *What's Happening!!*, was a part of our little group.

My mother and I lived with my grandmother, in her apartment on St. Nicholas Avenue. My earliest memories are of me sitting on the sofa next to my grandma, in the afternoon, as she nodded off while watching her "stories" on her black-and-white TV. Every time I tried to switch to *The Mickey Mouse Club*, she woke up and told me not to change the channel. I remember her scolding me for eating raw bacon and sticking my fingers in her Tom Collins drink mix and sneaking sweet potatoes straight from the can as she scooped them into the sauce pan.

My grandma was a slender, attractive woman, with long, curved fingernails that were always polished bright red. She moved slowly but with the grace and even occasional flair of a former dancer. As a young woman, she had lit up the floor in Harlem's Savoy Ballroom and kicked up her heels in numerous stage shows. In the early 1950s, she partnered with singer and band leader Billy Eckstine. By the time I came along, all that was ancient history. To me, she was Grandma.

Similarly, I did not know the extent of my mom's talent or versatility until much later in life, but others were aware of her talent and versatility. When movies shot in New York needed strong African American actors for roles, casting directors typically called Harlem's Al Fann Theatrical Ensemble for recommendations, and Chip Fields was always at the top of their list. She appeared in *Claudine*; *Come Back, Charleston Blue*; *Tough to Get Help*; and *The Taking of Pelham 123*. She could, and did, do everything: act, sing, dance, and even stunt work.

At some point, the two of us moved from my grandma's to the basement of the church where my mom took her acting classes, and then we moved again to an apartment on St. Nicholas Avenue, about two blocks from where we had started. We were poor, but I had no idea. I was loved, I always felt secure, and in that sense, I had everything I needed and more.

In 1975, my mom auditioned for a Broadway revival of the play *Hello, Dolly!* It starred the legendary Pearl Bailey, whose performance in a 1968 production featuring an all-black cast made her one of the all-time great Dolly Levis and earned her a Tony Award. This production was a mixed-race cast, a "flower garden," as Miss Bailey called it. Mom auditioned for the part of Minnie Fay in front of Miss Bailey herself. As she waited for word on whether to return the next day, the producer asked her to go to the Chinese restaurant across the street to get the star some soup.

My mom did not know whether she was being mistaken for an assistant or taken advantage of as she waited. Yet she ran the errand (because why not?) and then continued to wait at the theater, the soup she held for Miss Bailey passing from hot to warm to cold, mirroring her hopes for getting the job, as she sat there.

Finally, as night arrived and people began to go home, the producer came by, took the soup, and told my mom that she had made it to the next round. The following morning, several dozen prospective Minnie Fays lined up in a large rehearsal hall. As music played, everyone danced, and one by one they were dismissed. "Number three, thank you very much...Number twenty-seven, you can go. Thank you." There were several rounds of this. Debbie Allen was one of the finalists. So was my mom, who was not a trained singer or dancer, but just like in the play *A Chorus Line*, she needed that job. Oh God, she really needed that job.

And in the end, she was the only one left.

She was the new Minnie Fay—and it ended up changing her life, and ours.

* * *

The play opened in midsummer in Dallas and went on to Philadelphia, Chicago, Los Angeles, Boston, and the Kennedy Center Opera House in Washington, DC, before arriving at the Minskoff Theatre on Broadway. They did forty-two performances in New York, starting with three previews in early November. The theater critic in Boston praised the entire production, in particular my mom, and on opening night in New York, that glowing review was pasted onto a sandwich board in front of the Minskoff Theatre, with the part about my mom highlighted, thanks to Miss Bailey, who was extremely fond of her "little Chip."

As it turned out, my mom had brought my grandma to that opening night performance, and prior to the show, as she thanked Miss Bailey for her kind gesture, she also mentioned her mother was in the audience and that many years earlier she had actually been a backup dancer for one of Miss Bailey's nightclub shows. Mind you, they had been on the road for nearly six months, since July, and my mother had never brought this up. It got a look from Miss Bailey, one of those why-have-I-never-heard-this looks.

"Who's your mother?" she asked.

"Patsy Styles."

"Oh my God! You're Patsy's daughter!"

Three weeks later, my grandmother passed away. It was cancer. She had been a lifelong smoker.

My grandma was laid to rest on a Wednesday morning; my mom performed that afternoon in the matinee. Afterward, Miss Bailey sent her home in her personal limousine. To this day, my mom speaks about the special qualities Miss Bailey brought to the theater every night, onstage and off.

As I said, that play changed her life—and mine. When I think about the moment I decided I wanted to be an actor, I can honestly say that performing was in my blood. I only had to look as far as my grandmother and my mom. A door wasn't opened for me, but there was a path, and there were breadcrumbs on it. However, there was a particular moment, one I remember clearly. It happened when I visited my mom while she was on the road doing *Dolly!* Then it happened again backstage at the Minskoff on Broadway. Both times my mom's sister, my Aunt Pat, who, with my Uncle Lou, watched me when Mom couldn't, took me to these shows, and when we stepped through the backstage door, something special happened. I let go of her hand and looked around at the hustle and bustle of the actors and the crew getting ready for the performance, and I knew this was my life—or going to be someday.

Seeing this transformation happen right in front of me, with people like my mom and Miss Bailey and others coming in from the outside, from whatever they had been doing, from their regular lives, and turn themselves into other people who then created a different world, well, it was thrilling. It was magical.

It was the spark—me sensing who I was and what I was supposed to be.

One thing my mom learned while touring with *Dolly!* was that she loved Los Angeles and wanted to live there. No disrespect to Harlem, but in the mid-1970s, the city was not in one of its many heydays and my mom did not want to be there anymore. She did not want to raise her kid there either. She also sensed more opportunity for her as an actor in Los Angeles. Her friend Lawrence Hilton-Jacobs had moved there and landed *Welcome Back, Kotter*, and another close friend, Tim Pelt, the stepfather of Danielle Spencer, who played Dee in *What's Happening!!*, had also gone west. Both pals encouraged her to do the same.

So one day I came home from school at P.S. 92 and found our apartment all packed up. We did not have much, but everything we did have was in boxes, and Mom told me, "We're moving to California tonight."

My reaction?

Uh, okay.

I was a kid.

But that was it.

Goodbye, Harlem. Hello, Hollywood.

2

Commercial Girl

We arrived in Los Angeles and settled in a tiny apartment on Larrabee Street, in West Hollywood. Both of us were open to this new adventure. I attended West Hollywood Elementary School. Mom and I loved a joint on Sunset Boulevard called Power Burger. For free fun, we walked to Tower Records and spent hours sifting through the record bins and people-watching while listening to the latest hits piped through the store. On nice days, we hung out at West Hollywood Park. I won the park's annual Halloween costume contest dressed in a homemade costume as Groucho Marx. Mom and I jumped, squealed, and cried with joy. I think subconsciously it was validation for us that we didn't know we needed; she knew we didn't have much, I was self-conscious about wearing a costume my mom made.

Mom went on auditions, took classes, and booked commercials for Kentucky Fried Chicken and Pizza Hut. Each job, no matter how big or small, was a cause for celebration, but a national commercial was huge: We had money for rent, and then some. At some point, my mom decided I had a look and disposition that might get me some commercial or TV work, too. I met with Dorothy Day Otis, who headed up the top agency for children, and she signed me.

Days later, I went on my first audition, a commercial for Mrs. Butterworth's syrup. Since we did not have a car, my mom and I took the bus across town. As we settled into the orange fiberglass seats of the RTD bus, my mom made up a song, which I still remember: "Look out, world. Look out, hills. Here comes Chip and Kim Fields."

I was excited and hopeful as we walked into the casting office and checked in—that is, until I recognized the other girl waiting her turn. It was Janet Jackson, the baby sister of Michael and his brothers. I had seen her on the Jackson 5's summer TV special. She was sitting in a chair, dressed beautifully, and staring back at me.

I could not believe it.

I was starstruck.

Then reality kicked in. My smile disappeared, along with my enthusiasm for the tryout. This was my first audition, and she was Janet Jackson. My mom noticed the change in me. She took my little hand in hers, led me to the bathroom, sat me on the counter, and gave me a pep talk for the ages.

"Don't do that to yourself," she said. "Don't let anyone intimidate you or make you feel unsure or insecure about yourself. When your name is called, you go in there and know that you are the perfect you. If the casting people want something else, that's their choice. It does not reflect in any way on who you are or who else is sitting next to you. You show them confidence, baby. You show them pride. You show them Kim Fields."

Of course, it wasn't anything Janet was doing. It was all me, all in my mind. Ever been there? It's crazy how young insecurity or self-consciousness can creep up on us. That's why you have to catch it and don't let it take root.

The audition went well. The casting people liked my pigtails and smile. When my mom and I got back home, my new agent called and said the tape they had shot of me messed up and they wanted me to come back that afternoon for a reshoot. My mom said we'd be there, but it wasn't that simple. The bus didn't run at the right time and we didn't have the money for a taxi.

Undaunted, my mom grabbed her purse, took my hand, and we walked about a half mile to Santa Monica Boulevard, where she found us a clear patch of curbside and stuck out her thumb. We were not there for more than ten minutes before a man in a Porsche stopped for us—if you can picture that, this little black lady and her little black girl—and drove us to the address my mom gave him. He let us off in front of the building and wished us luck. Amazing, right? Then again, luck can often be seen in retrospect as a prayer that's been answered. Mom said, "God looks after fools, babies, and us."

I redid my audition and the next day found out that I'd booked the job. My mom and I screamed, hollered, jumped, danced, and cried—and then did it all over again like Jesus had come back and we were the only two going home with Him. It was the most exciting thing that had ever happened to me.

* * *

The Mrs. Butterworth's commercial ran nationally, and casting directors fell in love with my little face and my whack teeth. I scored TV ads for Frosted Flakes, Kraft barbecue sauce, and ALPO dog food, though the latter became my first disappointment and a lasting lesson in telling the truth. Here's what happened:

At the audition, I was asked if I liked dogs. I said, "Of course I like dogs." I was asked if I was afraid of dogs. "No, I'm not afraid," I said. Then came time to shoot; I was in front of the cameras and they let the dog out of his little kennel. He ran straight toward me and I turned and ran off the set. "I'm afraid!" I screamed. The director yelled, "Cut!" and they got another girl.

After Mom put together a string of guest spots on *Rhoda*, *What's Happening!!*, and several other TV shows, we moved to a kid-friendly neighborhood in Studio City. In the summer of 1977, she landed her biggest role to date, a three-episode arc on the series *Good Times*, and as was our routine, we hugged, danced, screamed, and cried. *Good Times* was a Norman Lear show, an imprimatur that made it important. It starred Jimmie Walker and Esther Rolle and was about a family living in a Chicago housing project. Although best known for J.J.'s catch-phrase *Dyn-o-mite!*, it was—like all of Norman Lear's shows—plugged into topical social issues.

Norman Lear absolutely adored my mom (he still does; I wish you could see how his face lights up and produces the warmest smile when he says her name). Until this book, I thought he loved her because he saw her in *Hello Dolly!* when she toured in LA. Ohhhh noooooo...Turns out, she auditioned for the role of Thelma on *Good Times*!!!! Yep. And the audition scene was J.J. and Thelma fighting over some money. In the audition, fearless Chip turned on her stunt-woman vibe and did some sort of flip and roll at Norman Lear's feet to get the money in the scene. That endeared her to him for their lifetimes. He even honored her by listening to her and giving a sibling singing group from New Jersey a shot on his hit series *What's Happening!!* Now, he wanted her to breathe dramatic life into what would become the iconic, abusive mother of Penny.

Mom's three episodes were about child abuse. She played a neighbor whose husband abandoned her after she got pregnant. Upset, her character loses control and abuses her ten-year-old daughter, played by Janet Jackson. The story line was important, powerful, and controversial. Knowing it was special, Mom wanted to get it right. She knew this was out of Janet's comfort zone, as it would be for any child actor, so she invited Janet to work on their scenes at our house.

For Mom, this was serious, intense work. But I could not imagine anything cooler or more surreal than Janet Jackson coming to our house. This was going to be a whole different experience than that first nerve-racking time I saw her. Try as I might, I had a nearly impossible time picturing my celebrity hero walking through our front door and saying hi to me.

A few days later, though, that's exactly what happened: Janet walked through our front door and said hi to me. Her big sister La Toya dropped her off. After a few moments, I was shooed away. But I was dying. Janet Jackson was in my house! I spied on them from the kitchen. Over the course of several weeks, I got used to Janet's presence. Sometimes La Toya stayed. But more often than not, she dropped Janet off and my mom and I took her back to her family's Tudor mansion in Encino.

Oh my gosh, I used to think as we waited for the guard to open the massive front gate that protected the house from fans who stood out front hoping to glimpse her brother Michael. I had a crush on Janet's youngest brother, Randy, and my eyes forever wandered in search of him. That made Janet laugh.

The Jacksons respected my mom, and they became friends of ours. Janet and I, in particular, became very good friends. Like a big sister, she taught me fun tween makeup and hair tips (putting eyeliner in the bottom rim of my eye and making tiny "kiss curls" with my hair near my ears). When I had a costume party, she let me wear one of her famous Mae West costumes from the family's TV show. Her generosity blew me away.

But her entire family was like that. Over the next few years, I visited their house many times and went swimming with her brothers and sisters. They embraced me as Janet's little friend. It was thrilling, nice, and eventually even normal.

I remember playing with Janet one day at her family's house when Michael was filming the movie *The Wiz*. We found the mold of the scarecrow mask in the Jacksons' bright yellow kitchen and toyed with the idea of making Jell-O in it. Both Janet and I thought that was so funny.

Once, I went to Disneyland with Janet and Michael. His chief of security drove us in a brown Rolls-Royce. Michael wore a hat and sunglasses, and that seemed to be enough to avoid getting recognized. The Enchanted Tiki Room musical attraction was his favorite. I remember laughing the entire day.

* * *

Our simple life of school, work, TV, and bed was interrupted when both my mom and I were hired on TV shows that shot in different places. Hers was a recurring role on the daytime soap *Days of Our Lives*, and I was cast on the new CBS sitcom *Baby, I'm Back*, starring Denise Nicholas and Demond Wilson as a man who reenters his family's life after abandoning them seven years earlier.

Since my mom couldn't be on the set with me, she asked my Aunt Pat and her husband, Lou, to move to LA, which they did. At home, she coached me through my scenes, though not like a stage mother. That was not her style of mothering or coaching. When we worked on scenes, she shared her insights and experience, but she was like her mentor, Pearl Bailey, who had patiently let Mom find her own way in *Hello, Dolly!*

Lots of work—that was my mom's thing. Hard work, learning, and faith in the process, that whatever it is you are trying to accomplish will work out the way it is supposed to. Those are the principles she taught me, until I got them, too—a little chip off the Chip.

But some lessons were impossible to accept. One day in September 1977, Mom learned her friend Tim Pelt was killed in a car crash on the Pacific Coast Highway. His stepdaughter and my playmate, Danielle Spencer, who costarred on *What's Happening!!*, was also seriously injured in the accident. I had never seen my mom that upset, and in turn, I was a bundle of raw emotion trying to understand something that was far beyond me. It was easier being an innocent kid.

3

Tootie

I had recently turned nine years old when I was invited to play Janet Jackson's friend on the show *Good Times*. The part seemed written especially for me. The producers knew me as Chip's daughter, they knew I was friends with Janet, and they had seen our rapport on the set. They even named the character "Kim."

After *Good Times*, I auditioned for a spin-off from *Diff'rent Strokes*, a new hit sitcom on NBC starring Charlotte Rae, Conrad Bain, Gary Coleman, Todd Bridges, and Dana Plato. However, outside the room where tryouts were held, I found myself the only African American among an assortment of cookie-cutter white girls, each one cuter and prettier than the other. *What am I doing here?* I thought.

My mom hauled me off to the bathroom for "the self-confidence pep talk" about how I shouldn't let anyone or anything intimidate me, and brought me back just as my name was being called. In the next room, I said hello to the casting director and several producers and read for the part of a girl named Tootie—"Dorothy 'Tootie' Ramsey." Afterward, I answered several questions, which generated some laughter, and left on the heels of someone saying, "You were great." Later, I heard it was love at first sight.

But there was one more audition—and a problem. Tootie was supposed to be twelve years old, and I was only nine. And "a small nine," as I had been called. Fortunately for me, executive producer Al Burton came up with a brilliant, silly, and maybe even borderline ridiculous idea.

"Can you roller-skate?" he asked.

I nodded and someone produced a pair of roller skates. I put them on and went for a spin around the sound stage. As I coasted back to the production table with my arms outstretched and a smile on my face, like an Olympic gymnast finishing her routine, I got a round of applause. I also got the job.

The episode, titled "The Girls School," was the last one of *Diff'rent Strokes*'s first season. TV insiders knew the network was giving Charlotte Rae her own show, an all-female version of *Welcome Back, Kotter* set in a boarding school, where her character, Edna Garrett, would be the housemother.

They cast seven girls as students, starting with Felice Schachter, who had been in the running for Dana Plato's part on *Diff'rent Strokes*, and Lisa Whelchel, a beautiful sixteen-year-old from Texas who could have doubled as a Miss America. The others—Julie Piekarski, Julie Anne Haddock, and Molly Ringwald—were all experienced child actors. Then there was Mindy Cohn, an ordinary kid with a big, ebullient personality who was spotted by Charlotte and one of the producers. I skated onto the scene toward the end of the casting process.

I was enamored of Julie Piekarski—or Julie Pie as I called her. Like Lisa Whelchel, she was a former Mouseketeer from *The All New Mickey Mouse Club*, which had been one of my favorite TV shows. Julie took me under her wing. Maybe it was because I was constantly standing *under* her wing. We were like sisters—one tall and blond, the other short and black.

The same thing happened with Mindy. On our first day on the set, she confided that she did not know what she was doing and hoped she would be funny. "Don't worry," I said. "I got your back." She had mine, too, and we have been that way for each other ever since. After the *Diff'rent Strokes* episode aired, NBC picked up our "backdoor pilot" as a series. They called it *The Facts of Life*.

We shot on the MetroMedia lot in Hollywood. Our set was near the soundstages for *Good Times*, *One Day at a Time*, *Diff'rent Strokes*, and *The Jeffersons*. I saw Janet Jackson in studio school; spied on my first crush, Todd Bridges; and met Roxie Roker's teenage son, Lenny Kravitz, a gorgeous high school freshman. Over the years I would see him around the studio. Lenny was hot even back then, and I was . . . well, I was maturing. I sent out the vibe and got nothing back except a smile, a pat on the hand, and reassurance that I was in the friend zone. *Ugh, have you no consideration of me outside the friend zone?* I thought. *None at all?*

Mikhail Baryshnikov was another hottie who captured our attention. During our first season, he filmed a TV special on the lot. He rehearsed next door to us, and we would take turns carefully opening the door a crack and sticking in our heads. We would've made excellent spies. We watched everything he did. He wore elegant clothes and always had a sweater draped over his shoulders. One day he walked into the bathroom and came out without his sweater. Instantly, Felice ran into the bathroom, fetched his sweater, and returned it to him. We were envious.

"What'd he say?"

"Thank you."

"But like how?"
"Like Baryshnikov."

* * *

The Facts of Life debuted at the end of summer 1979. Mrs. Garrett, everyone's favorite housekeeper, was now the house-mother at Eastland School, a private boarding school for girls. The first episode dealt with questions of sexual orientation and identity, and subsequent episodes, like all Norman Lear shows, addressed other issues, from divorce to smoking pot. But ratings were disappointing, and after only four episodes, the show went on a three-month break so the network could rework it.

That spring, *Facts* returned with nine more episodes, but again the ratings were lackluster. Instead of canceling the show over the summer, which would have been easy, the net-work went back to the drawing board yet again. We heard they were making "creative changes," and soon we learned those creative changes meant they were going to get rid of some of the girls.

I assumed that I was going to be among those let go, if not the first to go, because I was the only black girl. *They've got all these white girls in here,* I thought. *Of course they're going to stay. The black people always get cut first.* In the years since then, I have often wondered not why I thought that way, but what can I do to make sure my children never think that way. The answer is simple. Make sure there are roles for us. Make sure black kids see people like themselves on every size screen. Back then, it was me and Janet.

Needless to say, I was stunned when my mom told me that the show was getting ready to tape its second season, and I was still on it. I returned to work feeling excited but wary after learning that Julie Piekarski, Julie Anne Haddock, Felice Schachter, and Molly

Ringwald had been written out of the show. While they were brought back periodically, it was different and took getting used to. "Where'd everybody go?" Mindy asked.

In addition to whittling down the core group of girls, the producers also created a brand-new character, the streetwise, Bronx-born tomboy Jo Polniaczek. They cast Nancy McKeon in the role. Nancy was a perfect choice to play Jo. She had the look, the brains, and the heart. Nancy had worked in the business since she was two. She had done a ton of commercials, and her brother was on a series. The first time I saw her on the set, I recognized her from an episode of *The Love Boat*.

Nancy and I became friends right away. We were the only two in studio school. Lisa had taken an equivalency test to get her high school degree and did not have to go anymore, and Mindy continued to attend her private school. As I recall, her parents gave her permission to do the show but basically told producers, "You aren't going to mess around with her education."

For me, the big news was that I had grown taller and no longer had to wear roller skates. I had no idea, but parents around the country probably shared my delight. Years later, my *Living Single* costar Erika Alexander told me that she got in trouble for roller-skating in their house. When her parents asked what gave her the idea that roller-skating inside was okay, she said, "Tootie does it." Well, starting in season two, Tootie did not have to anymore. I was overjoyed to have my feet back.

Despite the cast changes, *Facts* retained its gutsy sensibility. The show continued to deal with serious issues, as we did in one of the early episodes that season when Tootie meets an African American boy who accuses her of only hanging out with white kids. I related to some of these story lines, but not all of them. I turned twelve toward the end of that season, and my social awareness, like my world itself, was fairly limited. *Here's your script. Learn your lines. Do well in school. Enjoy your childhood.*

My Aunt Pat drove me home, and I had dinner with my mom. I had posters of Todd Bridges and Michael Jackson on my bedroom walls. I watched *Wonder Woman*. I was not overly protected or sheltered, per se, but I worked and so I had very little awareness of the impact *Facts of Life* was having on girls across the country or that I was becoming a role model for other little black girls, until about three-quarters of the way through the second season.

Suddenly the fan mail the network delivered to me increased from a few letters to a box to several large bags full. Of course, this reflected the show's rise in the ratings. *Facts* climbed from number seventy-four to twenty-nine and was NBC's highest-rated comedy and the second-most-popular show on their 1980–1981 schedule. The changes the network made to the show had worked. We were a hit, but for whatever reason, I never felt like it. I think the other girls shared my sentiments. We were just there, chugging away.

Outside, beyond the studio gates, we were recognized, which took getting used to. I got scared when Todd Bridges and I were riding in the Watts Christmas Parade as co–grand marshals, and screaming girls tried to pull him out of the car. But I just got screams. "Tootie! Tootie! I love you." The love was amazing. My mom kept me grounded though. When I first booked *The Facts of Life* and then at the start of every season, she stood in front of me like a coach at the start of football season and gave me a mini-lecture.

"Baby, you start at one hundred percent," she said, pointing her right arm straight up to twelve o'clock. "Every day that you are on the set or out in public interacting with people, you can either stay at one hundred percent or you can do or say things that chip away at that number." She let her arm drop a bit, first to two o'clock and then to four. "It's all about the way you behave, the way you speak to other people, the way you treat other people. It's very easy to slip.

"But it's even easier to stay at one hundred percent. Remember that your entire life. It's up to you."

She was right.

4

Growing Up

W ow, look at you."
 That was the greeting I got from everyone when I
showed up to start the show's third season. The same was
even more true for others. Lisa was closing in on twenty years
old and without makeup and a school uniform, she looked
more like the gorgeous young woman she was than a high
school student. Mindy and Nancy were no longer kids, and
lest anyone wonder the status of cute little Tootie, well, the
obvious was tackled in the opening scene of the season premiere when she flashes her braces and declares, "I'm a
teenager."

Though in real life I was not yet a teenager, I was, like my
cast mates, exhibiting the signs of burgeoning young adulthood. At the end of the previous season, my mom had bought
me a training bra—bright pink! But there was no training those
girls. We were barely back to work on season three when one of
the show's female producers came into the wardrobe room and

said they wanted to hide my boobs. The suggestion of "taping me down" came up but was vetoed fairly quickly.

Honestly, I had a harder time with those horrific sweaters and strange gauchos they had me wear to make me look young and perky. I wanted to look cool—and knew I didn't.

Going through puberty on television was not fun. I handled getting braces no problem. But the emotional swings of changing hormones, getting my period, and looking in the mirror and seeing boobs and curves that were not there the previous week, or the previous day, all the while knowing I had to spend the day in front of a camera took getting used to. Looking back, I can say growing up is a task and I was just starting.

As I emerged from this cocoon of being a little kid, Nancy was still my go-to. We were together in studio school, but she was in high school and already handling womanhood. She was dating and learning how to drive. I sat in the backseat of her car while she went through driver's education. I called her for advice the day I decided to shave my legs for the first time. My mom and I had moved to a little house in Burbank, and I was in the bathroom, holding a pink razor in one hand and a portable phone in the other. Nancy talked me through both legs.

My costars were a great bunch. There was no fighting, pulling pranks, no egos run amok or sneaking behind the soundstage for a cigarette, and there was a reason for that. The people who were part of our lives during those years, our parents and extended families of grandmas, aunts, and uncles, were all good people who made sure that we developed into good people, too.

Aunt Pat was my guardian on set until I was eighteen. Every year my mother made sure I never allowed anyone to overlook her. "People get caught up in satisfying the star," she said. "You'll ask for a piece of gum and they'll bring you a plate with fourteen different flavors because they have to make you happy. Everyone's job is tied to the show, and the kid has to be happy. But that production assistant or producer doesn't think about getting lunch for the person taking care of the kid. They don't consider that the kid doesn't drive themselves to the set."

As my mom talked, she inched closer to me, her voice growing softer, until she was right in my face. "Baby, make sure you never let them overlook Aunt Pat. When people are introduced to you, a lot of times they will only see the famous kid on the TV show. It's on you to say, 'This is my Aunt Pat.'"

I understood. When I guested on *Diff'rent Strokes*, I saw firsthand the show's star, Gary Coleman, go off on the director and thought, *Oh, this is what my mother means when she says how not to act.* I heard grownups describe Gary as rude—and worse. Dana Plato, God bless her, one of that show's other child stars, was difficult in a whole other way. Once she came to work with her hair dyed pink, which caused issues when it could not be washed out. I remember thinking, *Honey, you're on a TV show. What are you doing?*

If my mother heard even a hint of attitude in my voice, she put her hand up like a traffic cop and said, "You're walking around like your behind weighs a ton." I'm often asked how I stayed sane and grounded growing up a child actor. My answer? My mom. She never stopped being a parent. One time I didn't clean my room and when she sent me back to clean it, I asked, "Isn't that why we have a housekeeper?" My mom immediately got *Facts of Life* executive producer (and parent) Al Burton on the phone and said, "Kim will no longer be part of your TV show because she doesn't know how to handle it." He played along and I fell in line.

Luckily, I was a good kid: even-tempered, obedient, respectful, and happy. In fact, in the episode that season where Mrs. Garrett tells Tootie she cannot go to Jermaine Jackson's concert after he personally invited her, I had to be coached on how to talk back and lose my temper. My mom actually helped me with that script. Today, that seems funny and obviously ironic: going to your mom to learn how to be impertinent. I always went to Mom for coaching on more demanding material like working on the TV movie *Children of Divorce* as an alcoholic gymnast. She worked with me until she sensed I was at the right place and then said, "Okay, you got it?"

That was our groove. She never wanted me to be one of those cute, precocious child stars who smiled and said lines that were beyond their years in that annoying, unkind way. She took her craft seriously and wanted me to embrace it in the same way. I tried—and I tried—and hoped to be at her level one day.

* * *

I was nearly thirteen when my mom let me know there was going to be a major change in our lives. "We're going to have a baby," she said as her boyfriend, John, stood with his arm around her, both of them watching my reaction. I screamed with excitement and hugged them as hard as I could. I had been an only child for my entire life and was thrilled at the prospect of being someone's big sister.

She worked throughout her pregnancy and looked to be all belly—the same, my Aunt Pat said, as when she carried me. On the night she went into labor, we were watching a Lakers basketball game on TV. "Is it time?" John and I kept asking; after several hours, my mom finally said, "It's time!" I remember a discussion on whether to put plastic garbage bags in the front seat of John's car in case Mom's water broke; it didn't. I went to work the next morning and was between scenes when Aunt Pat said it was time to go to the hospital.

At the Tarzana Medical Center, I pitched a hot-as-fish-grease fit when the nurse said I was too young to be in the delivery room. "Why does John get to be in there with all the doctors and nurses and not me?" I said. "I'm the sister!" But all was forgotten later that afternoon, March 1, 1982, with the arrival of a beautiful baby girl named Alexis. I was immediately ushered in to meet my sister, whose perfect face and tiny little hands and feet inspired me to gush, "She's the cutest thing I've ever seen."

Two months later, I officially became a teenager. For my thirteenth birthday, my mother surprised me with a talent show–themed celebration. Mindy Cohen did stand-up comedy, and Michael Damien, the new heartthrob on *The Young and the Restless*, got down on one knee and sang a romantic ballad directly to me. Then, during the instrumental break, he took my hand, pulled me close, and slow danced me around the room. You could have bought me for a penny and asked for change.

The party ended when *One Day at a Time* actor Glenn Scarpelli, one of my dear friends, did a riotously funny striptease down to his boxers to Olivia Newton-John's hit "Physical." My favorite gift? An alarm clock from my friend and crush, Todd Bridges. He was a cool, laid-back guy, without an ounce of jerk in him, and my idea of *wow, he's perfect.* We had known each other for years. We posed together for the cover of *Right On!* magazine. For my twelfth birthday, he gave me a Rick James album, and a year later, when I unwrapped his gift and found an alarm clock and saw it was already wound, I thought, *Oh God, he loves me!*

Like Lenny, Todd flung me into the dreaded and disappointing friend zone. At work, my older costars were dating and trading stories about boys, causing me to literally ache for someone special to notice me in the same way. Love was in the air that summer when we spent three weeks in Paris, shooting a *Facts of Life* TV movie. I remember Lisa coming back from a walk through the Tuileries and telling a reporter that she wished her boyfriend were there to share it all with her. Me, I had my Walkman with me, and Rick Springfield in my ears, and a question in my head: *When would I have that special boy in my life?*

It happened later that fall. His name was Harold "P" Pruitt, and he was my first real but very innocent boyfriend. I met him through my mom's repertory company. A proponent of giving back, she always looked for empty theaters in the community or a rec center where she could hold classes and put up a show. "P" was a kid in one of her classes. Malcolm-Jamal Warner was also in this repertory company. I wouldn't know until decades later that at that time, Malcolm had a crush on me.

P and I went to the movies. He was my first kiss, my first let's-take-a-walk-and-hold-hands, and the first boy I needed to call at night to tell him what had happened in my day. Starting the fourth season, *The Facts of Life* moved to the Universal Studios lot, where I was given my own dressing room trailer, which I decorated with posters of Todd Bridges and Michael Jackson, and several times P visited me on the set. During breaks, we strolled around the studio lot, holding hands as we peeked inside the storied soundstages.

Ah, yes, that first boyfriend, those first kisses—like a smile that lasted all day. It was fun.

* * *

Not so fun for the *Facts of Life* cast was being a target of parodies and cheap humor. We did not appreciate *Mad* magazine's satire, "The Yaks of Life." The six-page spread, in the December 1982 issue of the humor magazine, seemed mean, though not nearly as mean as comedian Joan Rivers when she mocked us as "the Fats of Life." Given that she was raising her own teenage daughter, Joan should have known better than to make fun of young, developing women that way.

I was dealing with sensitive weight and body issues, and

putting it out there as she did was unnecessary and hurtful on many levels. Apparently somebody with influence heard the comedian and decided she had a point. One day we returned from a break and found the chips and cookies and yummy snack food at the craft services table had been replaced with celery, carrots, jicama, and other vegetables. They brought in a scale and made us all weigh in each week. Lisa was also sent to several so-called fat camps and someone from the network suggested I see a therapist. When I asked why, I was told, "Because of your eating."

I remember turning to my Aunt Pat. "Do I eat a lot?" I asked. The network exec jumped in. "Maybe you feel bad or are worried about something and don't realize it. A therapist will help you figure that out." I shook my head. "No, I'm just hungry," I said. "I'm short and busty, and I don't exercise or play a sport. But I'm still hungry."

They were more enlightened when it came to my hair. Tootie started out in pigtails, but a single hairstyle does not serve a young girl for long, and the show's producers, recognizing that I had different hair than the other girls, hired a brilliant and experienced stylist for me. Her name was JoAnn Stafford-Chaney. She has since won an Emmy and worked on movies with Will Smith and Denzel Washington, but back in the day she was building her reputation as TV's go-to stylist for African American women. She really knew black girl hair, plain and simple, and I was the very appreciative beneficiary of her expertise.

In the early days of the series, when I had a zigzag part in my hair, it was because I had hair breakage. Thank goodness for JoAnn. She figured out a way to treat that problem in a healthy manner and keep my hair in good condition. She also kept me in line with the most current styles, telling me the latest ways black girls my age were wearing their hair; and since my hair was done three out of every four weeks a month that *Facts* shot, I spent a lot of time with her, asking questions and listening.

In terms of fashion and looks, I rarely saw other young black girls featured in the teen magazines, which made finding answers to my many questions about growing up more difficult than it is nowadays with the Internet. If I could go back and hang out with my teenage self, I would give her a gigantic, loving hug and tell her to look past her concerns about clothes and hair and see the hottie inside her.

"Dear Teenage Kim, People come in all different shapes, sizes, and shades, and the older Kim is not going to magically get any taller, so the younger Kim should not try to change things beyond her control. Don't stand in front of your mirror for an hour wishing you could add six inches. It ain't going to happen. In fact, over time, you'll see some of your peers obsess about their physical appearance at the expense of their soul—and in some cases their life. As you grow up, you need to understand it is the goodness inside people that makes them attractive and hot, and, girl, you got a ton of that goodness, so focus on making sure that little light of yours shines bright. Nurture that potential to do good and you will be good.

"Your shyness and awkwardness is normal, but don't use that as an excuse to avoid the excitement of trying new things. It is normal to be curious. Don't be stupid, but take chances. Yes, you will make mistakes, but you will learn from them. You will fail and fall down, but you will get back up and try again. That is called living life—and that, my younger self, is what you are supposed to do.

"You're supposed to live.

"And P.S.—I do not know if the braces were necessary. A slight overbite can be sexy.

"And P.S.S.—Without giving anything away, things work out.

"And P.S.S.S.—Don't bother trying to look cute for George Clooney when he joins *The Facts of Life* for season seven. Once again, you will be tossed into the Lil Sis Zone, the cute, sweet pal pile, before you can blink."

5

The Teenager

At fourteen years old, I went into my bathroom to look at myself in the mirror. I wanted to see if I looked different. I studied my face, looked deeply into my eyes, smiled, frowned, stepped back, and leaned so close my nose almost touched the glass. I didn't see anything new. But something had changed. God had entered my life and I could feel His presence. I was checking for visible signs. I wondered if other people could see.

The transformation happened about a month earlier when my mom and I visited a few local churches that were supporting a faith-friendly play she had written and directed. One Sunday, as I was listening to a service at one of the churches—it may have been Ward AME Church in South-Central Los Angeles—I discovered my faith. It wasn't a Saul-to-Paul moment, but I felt it happen then and there, and if I close my eyes right now, I can still feel that visceral change. It was like being swept up by a wave that was all warmth, comfort, and love, and it never stopped.

From that moment on, I felt a steady pull toward the Word

of God. This change could've caused confusion, I suppose, but I accepted it as natural and normal. Maybe not for everyone, but for me. I spoke to my mom and my pastor and came to understand what had happened. I'd been born again, this time as a Christian. I began to pray regularly and discovered a relationship with the Lord that seemed as if it had always been there, waiting for me to discover it. In a sense, I suppose that's exactly what had happened.

Trusting in His plan helped me understand that some of life made sense, while other parts would always be a mystery, but His love could keep me centered and grounded through good and bad times. Even at my relatively young age, I could comprehend all that information because, as it was explained to me, God and all His infinite wisdom and everything I would read in the Bible and hear in church could all be boiled down to one simple concept—love.

I got it—and life went on.

Later that year, I had a harder time understanding the invitation I received to go into the recording studio and cut a song. As I laughingly said to my mom, that was a mystery. I wasn't a singer. There was a little girl named Shanice Wilson who participated in a few of my mom's productions, and she had a voice that literally stopped the shows. At nine, she sang in a commercial with Ella Fitzgerald, and a few years later she released the first of many albums. She *was* a singer. I was not.

But I could carry a tune very well and was game to try. Hal Davis, one of the all-time great Motown songwriters, had contacted my mom about getting me to rerecord "Dear Michael," a song he and Elliot Willensky had written for Michael Jackson's second solo album, *Forever, Michael*, in 1975. Now, Michael was on top of the charts—and the world—with his megahit album *Thriller*, and the idea was for me to record this new version of "Dear Michael" as if I were representing all the girls my age who had a crush on him.

I studied a rough version of the song prior to the recording session. It featured a scratch vocal by a professional singer, and I remember thinking, *I don't sound like that.* In the studio, I said as much to Mr. Davis, who told me not to worry and just sing the best I could. They would do multiple takes, he explained, and stack my vocals, layering one version on top of another to make my voice sound fuller and richer. That sounded cool and helped me relax.

Though my voice was strictly untrained and barely rehearsed, the song, released in mid-1984, went to number fifty-five on Billboard's R&B chart. It was considered a hit. I promoted it on *American Bandstand* and *Soul Train*, shows I watched religiously, and to this day when I come across YouTube clips of myself on *Bandstand*, I think, *Oh my gosh, that girl is so terrified.* And I was. I wore a black vest with some sparkles over a red silk shirt and black pants, and pulled my hair in the fab '80s hairstyle, very kid-appropriate. My nerves did not show when I lip-synced the lyrics, but after, when I stepped forward to speak with *Bandstand*'s legendary host, Dick Clark, I was barely able to focus. "How old are you?" he asked.

Suddenly I went brain-dead. "Me?" I asked. He nodded. "Yeah." We were the only two onstage, and I was the only one with a microphone pointed at me. "I'll be fifteen on May twelfth," I said. People applauded—probably because they were relieved I did not pass out.

I was more confident when, a short time later, Mr. Davis took me back into the studio, this time to record a more disco-and dance-oriented song Mr. Willensky had written called "He Loves Me, He Loves Me Not." I knocked out the vocals in one afternoon and geared up for something I did not do with the previous single: a photo shoot.

My mom served as the stylist and drew inspiration from Madonna's "Material Girl," a massive hit at the time. She dressed me in a pink catsuit with a white lace tank top, white lace skirt, white lace gloves, and a white lace bandana in my hair, and stood me in front of a paint-splattered backdrop. There were flowers and rose petals everywhere. It was a gorgeous motif, colorful and fresh, but with one little thing looking out of place. In the lower right hand corner, there was a wok. That's right, a Chinese cooking wok.

The record cover folded out to a poster, but if you didn't unfold it you never saw it. But during the shoot, my mother thought the composition of me, the dress, the shower of pink, red, and white rose petals cried out for something metallic. She hurried through the studio and came back with a wok, which she set down in the foreground. To this day, it doesn't make sense. We just say, "Hey, it was the '80s."

* * *

When my new song turned into an even bigger hit than my first single, climbing to number twenty-two on the U.S. dance charts, my "music team" put together a band, added several more songs to create an act, and we were booked as entertainment on a Hawaiian cruise. I did that twice. I also toured on the Christian music circuit. My most memorable gig was a showcase in front of a packed house at the Tropicana in Hollywood, but only because of what happened before I went onstage.

Earlier that day, I had taped the game show *Body Language*. Fellow teen actor Jason Bateman, then of *Silver Spoons* and *It's Your Move* fame, was the other celebrity guest, and while we knew each other in passing from working at the same studio, we had a good time playing the game together. Before saying goodbye, I invited him to my show. Cut to Jason walking into my dressing room right before I went onstage, smiling and saying how excited he was for me and to be there. Without saying much else, we embraced and shared a sweet teenage kiss. It was a one-time thing, but God, I've never forgotten the perks of pop stardom.

There were other perks, too—like competing on the *Battle of the Network Stars*. This competition series, which pitted stars from the three broadcast TV networks in athletic events, was one of those shows that I never missed, so I was ecstatic when I was invited to be on team NBC.

I did the show twice that year, in May and December. It was shot on the athletic field at Pepperdine University's picturesque campus in Malibu, and I discovered that I was a fierce competitor. I did not want to lose. I realized this while running a relay race we needed to win to move into first place. I heard my teammates—Michael J. Fox, Mark Harmon, Vicki Lawrence, and Lisa Whelchel—cheering and urging me to go faster, and I willed myself to whiz pass the other actress who had the lead.

In retrospect, I realize something else may have also motivated me to run faster: the prospect of getting a victory hug from Mark Harmon. Clearly my interests were changing. But there was more. Halfway through that next season of *Facts*, Nancy graduated from high school and left studio school, which meant I faced the prospect of being in the classroom by myself. I didn't see that happening; as far as I was concerned, Nancy and I were ride-or-die together. As a result, I chose to attend my local public school, Burbank High.

I started midway through my junior year, and though I had to work around my *Facts of Life* schedule, it was the perfect decision for me. It was the school experience I'd fantasized about. I had my own locker, a full schedule of classes, and new friends. I had the best of both worlds—work I loved and a normal life. I did homework, attended school events, took the SATs and ACTs, and met friends after school for burgers and Cokes.

I also got involved in student government and proposed an appreciation week for our school's custodians. "This is the way my mom raised me," I explained to the principal when asking permission to stage the event. "Don't overlook the taken-for-granted." The principal asked, "Do you think the custodians here are taken for granted?" I said, "Have the students here ever said thank you to the custodians for keeping the school clean?" I made my point and produced the event, which still ranks among my proudest achievements.

Then everything got more complicated: I met a boy. His name was Loy, and we went to the same church. Already sixteen, he played quarterback on his high school's varsity football team in Pasadena. He was *that* guy—handsome, funny, and athletic.

When we went out, he always came into the house and said hello to my mom and played with Alexis. Big points. My friends liked him, too. We talked daily and I was happiest when I was hanging out with him. I did not lose myself in him, as some girls do when they have a boyfriend. My life was too busy and full for that. But I enjoyed having someone fall for me, and really like me. It made up for all those moments when I struggled to like myself because I was too short, too heavy, too busty, or too much of something else I would rather have changed.

Then came this boy who didn't want anything changed. We talked every day and night, about everything. Little things became incredibly important. Like I was miserable when I could not attend his homecoming game because I was supposed to be in a play my mom was producing that same Saturday night, and she insisted I honor my commitment to the play. I cried to Loy on the phone. "She doesn't get it! She doesn't understand me."

Oh, but my mom showed just how much she got it when Loy invited me to his school's prom. The dance was everything to me, as it is to so many girls. I bought a pink *Gone with the Wind* meets *Desperately Seeking Susan*–style gown with a matching hat and gloves, and Loy rented a formal tux with tails and a shawl collar. Every conversation was about the evening, and my mom seemed to want to make it special. "I'm so happy for you," she said. "So I'll book the car for you for the night."

On prom night, Loy came over to our house and the car my mother arranged for pulled up right on time. It was a vintage Rolls-Royce, and we were thrilled to see this luxurious carriage waiting for us in front of the house. I saw the chauffeur, poised beside the open back door, and thought, *Even better.* But as we got closer, I recognized the driver was a close family friend. My smile faded and I looked at my mom, who smiled. "I booked the car—*and* the driver," she said.

As for driving, it was on my agenda. One of my favorite *Facts of Life* episodes is "Tootie Drives," which aired midway through the seventh season, and the script, by future Academy Award–winner Paul Haggis, had all the girls taking turns teaching Tootie how to drive. It was not far from the truth. While all of my *Facts* costars offered encouragement, my mom actually let me learn on her sleek Mercedes sedan. My Aunt Pat flat out refused no matter how much I pleaded I needed the practice. "No, let your mother take you," she said. I think the word *practice* freaked her out.

In the meantime, every morning I drove to the studio while my mom sat stoically in the passenger seat. I think her eyes were shut. Though every once in a while, as I pulled off the freeway and onto Forest Lawn Drive, she calmly said, "Baby, can you get me out of the bushes, please. The road is to your left." (For the record, I got my driver's license on my first try.)

* * *

Once school ended, I planned to take it easy all summer. I wanted to play with my adorable little sister, Alexis, and hang out with Loy; that was it. Of course that proved unrealistic. One day, Loy drove me to my orthodontist appointment. There, my orthodontist, after poking around my mouth, found a problem. According to him, my braces were sending and receiving radio signals from a foreign country—one that was unfriendly to the United States. Sensing a setup, I turned to Loy. "Did my mom put you up to this so I wouldn't kiss you?"

As Loy shook his head no, the doctor placed a hideous, helmetlike contraption on my head, explaining it would block the radio signals. "Is this for real?" I asked. It wasn't. A moment later, I heard a voice through a hidden earpiece in the helmet. "Hi, Kim, this is Dick Clark, and you're on *Bloopers & Practical Jokes*." I laughed harder than everyone.

Later that summer, there was more activity, but of a serious nature: breast reduction surgery. For more than a year, I had been asking to have the surgery and put an end to the constant pain I was in. My back hurt from the time I got out of bed until I lay back down again at night. Finally, my mom, after speaking with doctors and friends, came around, found a top plastic surgeon in Santa Monica, and arranged for the procedure.

I'd had surgery only one other time, an emergency appendectomy when I was twelve years old. So I was nervous as my mom drove me to the plastic surgeon's office, but eager for the change. After a brief exchange with the doctor about what to expect, I kissed my mom and woke up several hours later with my chest wrapped in layers of thick, white surgical dressing.

"You're going to feel tightness for a while," the surgeon explained after I was more awake. "Those are the bandages. Later tonight and over the next few days, there might be some pain. But that will go away, and then I think you will be very happy."

Recovery took about a week and a half, and when I removed the dressing and stood in front of the mirror, I had one of those big "wow" moments. I was noticeably smaller, thank goodness, and in better proportion for my body (yes!). Most importantly, as my body healed, I was no longer in constant pain. A weight had been lifted from my shoulders, literally.

The transformation was nearly complete. Boyfriend. Driver's

license. Braces off. Boobs fixed. It was, in retrospect, the kind of checklist that gives parents nightmares. Certainly it was no coincidence that this new, more grown-up and independent phase of my teenage life inspired my mom to give me *the talk*—or her version of the talk, which I refer to as "The Godfather Sex Talk."

One day, after I finished my homework, she called me into her bedroom and motioned for me to sit at the edge of the bed. "Do you remember the movie *The Godfather?*" she asked. I nodded, as she knew I would, since we had watched it together, with my mom providing commentary and insight on the amazing acting. "Do you remember when Michael Corleone got with his wife, the Italian girl, the one before Diane Keaton?" I nodded. "Well, remember their wedding night? After the ceremony and the celebration, they're in their villa, and the way she brings her arm across her body to reveal herself, and the way Michael looked at her?" Her voice rose, turning this description into a question, to which I again nodded, curious to see where she was taking this talk. "That's how you want your husband to look at you."

Finished, my mom waited for a reaction from me. I held it together, letting her know I had understood the message. The young Corleone bride was only looked at in that special way because she was innocent and pure. Michael was going to be the first and only one to have been with her. But I could not believe her unique approach to this uncomfortable rite of passage, and finally I lost it. I cracked up. "Did you really just use *The Godfather* for our sex talk?" I asked.

She nodded—and I hugged her.

"I love it," I said. "And I love you."

6

The Senior

My senior year was not supposed to start this way. Like a patient listening to a bad diagnosis, I sat motionless on the sofa, light-headed and numb, taking in all the gruesome details. Loy had cheated on me with another girl, actually a friend of mine, which was even worse. As far as I was concerned, that was it. Our relationship ended then and there.

My heart was shattered. I was one of those girls who fell in love hard, and now that it was over, I fell apart. My mom cradled me in her arms and said, "You will be okay." I cried for days. I couldn't concentrate. I moped around, lost and unable to focus. "This is just one of those things we all go through, baby," my mom said, trying to comfort me. "It doesn't get easier. But it will get better."

I found that hard to believe, but she was right. I stuck around home until *Facts* started the new season. I played with my sister. I participated at church and volunteered at functions. I went fishing with my Uncle Luther at Castaic Lake, one time catching two bass and boasting that I had put the worms on the hook myself. I inherited my first car, our beat-up Honda Accord. After the radio broke, I used three-year-old Alexis's plastic Fisher-Price cassette player and rotated through my three essential tapes: Sade, Commissioned, and The Winans. I guested on several Dick Clark specials, including one where my old friend Malcolm-Jamal Warner and I shared a brief kiss. (He says *I* kissed *him* because it sounds better to him to recall it that way.) And gradually, I found, as so many of us do, that with time, my heart proved more resilient than I thought.

At school, I loaded up on activities. I was elected student body vice president. I managed the baseball team. I participated in mock trial. I enjoyed geometry, history, and science. Thanks to an inspiring biology teacher, I thought about becoming a marine biologist. I didn't know Jodie Foster, but the former child star, who'd been raised by a single mother and had gone to Yale, served as a role model from afar.

Like her, I knew I was going to go college, which would make me the first in my family to do so, but I hadn't decided where or what I would study. I fantasized about going away to either Evangel University, a Christian school in Missouri, or to San Diego State. But because I was still doing *Facts*, I had to stay in LA. So I applied to Pepperdine University—and prayed.

I had fallen in love with the Pepperdine campus when we lived in Malibu and while taping *Battle of the Network Stars* there. It was nestled in the green hills above Malibu, with breathtaking views of the Pacific Ocean. On a tour of the campus, I asked if anyone went to class—it was that beautiful. I also noticed the diversity of the student body. People of every color, shape, size, and type crisscrossed the campus the day I was there. It looked like they could be my friends.

The school's Christian affiliation was also a key factor. Faith was encouraged, not frowned upon. It was studied, discussed, appreciated, celebrated, explored, and practiced out in the open, and that was the way I approached my faith. In early January, I came home to find a large envelope waiting for me. With my mom standing nearby, I ripped it open. Apparently my GPA, test scores, personal essay, and prayers had worked. I was in. Of course, you know how we celebrated. No matter what we're celebrating, it's always screams, jumping up and down, and tears.

With the pressure off, the rest of the school year zipped by. At the homecoming football game, we played our crosstown rival John Burroughs High. I helped make posters and put them up all over school. *Go Burbank!* We won the game 14 to 10 and celebrated late into the night. At lunch the next day, I convinced a few of my cheerleader friends to drive to Burroughs with me and flaunt our victory. We taped posters to the side of my Honda, cruised their parking lot, and yelled our cheers through open windows. The Burroughs kids bombarded us with food. A cheeseburger flew smack into the side of my face. I felt naughty—and loved it.

Only one thing went missing that year: a boyfriend. I put out the vibe that I was available, but it went unanswered, something that still mystifies me. I had lots of guy friends, but none of them took that next step. I do not think anyone was intimidated. Nor was I unfriendly, inaccessible, distant, or stuck-up. Was it possible I was too nice? Maybe I didn't fit a type. I was not the peppy cheerleader or one of the girls in the bathroom doing their makeup and hair. Nor was I edgy or naughty. I was me: accessible, open, funny, interested, curious, and scrappy.

For whatever reason, though, none of that was right. The boys liked me, but apparently not as girlfriend material.

Interesting the way that stuff stays with you.

Maybe you know what I mean.

Ugh.

But what could I do? That was the reality. When it came time for the senior prom, I was left looking for a date. At the eleventh hour, I asked a family friend to take me. Though he was a few years older than me, he was a good sport and helped me through a sensitive time. In fact, I had a good time.

When the yearbook was released, I was honored that my classmates had voted me Most Talented. I still treasure that recognition. Then, before I knew it, came graduation. Our theme was "Take a Look at Me Now," and I was one of the student speakers. I worked on my speech for weeks, trying to summon all of my accumulated teen wisdom in a scant three minutes. I used the analogy of the metamorphosis of a caterpillar to a butterfly to show our transformation over our high school years. In the end, here's what I dropped on my fellow graduates: "Remember when we were kids? We'd see butterflies and say, 'Mommy, Daddy, look at the butterfly!' Well, Mom, Dad . . . take a look at me now!"

While "drop the mic" wasn't the catchphrase then that it is now, I sure did flap my graduation gown as I took my seat like I nailed it, a.k.a. like I dropped the mic. I wanted to leave my schoolmates inspired, full of hope, proud of their metamorphoses into young adults (which wasn't easy for any of us, was it?), and ready to go get what the future had for them. The cool thing was, I really felt that way.

My Voice

7

The College Girl

What's that saying about making plans? Well, it happened to me. Instead of starting school in the fall, I deferred enrollment when the *Facts of Life* producers scheduled production of a two-hour movie special, starting in the middle of summer, June and July 1986. This was our first movie special since Paris, which had been an exciting, broadening, and educational experience. This time we were headed to Australia. It made all my talk about going off to college a bit anticlimactic, but you heard no complaints from me.

The three-week trip Down Under began in July. Between shooting, Mindy, Nancy, Lisa, and I visited the Sydney Opera House, climbed Ayers Rock, and ventured into the outback in Alice Springs, where, as part of Mindy's and my story line in the movie, we spent time in an aboriginal village. Yes, it was cutesy, clichéd stuff, but I felt privileged to meet and learn about the country's indigenous people.

Above everything was the time I spent with the crew. I was already a "crew baby," meaning that whenever I had free time on the *Facts* set back home, I sat on the cameras, the boom, and near all the other equipment, and asked how things worked. I shadowed the crew. I wanted to learn—and on a set, no group is more eager and willing to share their knowledge and skill set than the crew. In Australia, I found a talented, patient instructor and friend in John Mahaffie, our camera operator and second unit director. A charismatic New Zealander, John, who went on to work with writer-director Peter Jackson, let me sit at his feet, carry a camera case, and tag along whenever he went on location to shoot with the second unit. By the end of the trip, I'd had a master class on composition and lighting. It shaped my eye forever.

After the movie wrapped, we returned home and went straight into production on the show's eighth season. Charlotte Rae had left at the end of the previous season to pursue other projects at a slower pace—or rather at her own pace. Enter Academy Award–winner Cloris Leachman, whose credits included *The Mary Tyler Moore Show* and her own spinoff, *Phyllis*. The handoff between the two brilliant actresses occurred in the emotional two-hour season opener, as Edna Garrett turned over the keys of her general store, Over Our Heads, to her sister, Beverly Ann.

My eyes were full of tears as Charlotte took her final bow. In my opinion, her work on the show had been overlooked. Though the public mainly saw the four girls, and so much of the writing was about us girls, the show belonged to her. An enormously talented actor, she made it look easy, which is not generally the case when working with kids and comedy. I felt immense gratitude.

As for Cloris, I was a big fan of hers from the classic Mel Brooks comedy *Young Frankenstein*. I knew that movie inside and out. On the day we met, I had to prevent myself from screaming like Frau Blücher, "He vas my boyfriend." To her credit, Cloris did not try to rebuild or renovate our house to suit her. She respected that it was already built. As an actress, she was physical and liked working with props. She wanted something in her hands. Sometimes that made the director a little nutty, but she was Cloris-*freaking*-Leachman—and more, she was really funny.

Speaking of funny, George Clooney joined our *Facts* family full time that season, building upon a guest-starring arc from the previous season. *Facts* was his first regular gig as an actor and my heart warms every time I hear him talk about those early days in his career, because he does it with fondness, appreciation, and affection. Yes, he is Hollywood's biggest leading man, and one of the nicest leading men, but back then, in the mid-1980s, he was an up-and-coming actor with a winning grin and a messy mane of dark curls. His dad was a local news anchor and way more famous than him, and his aunt, of course, was the singer Rosemary Clooney, which I thought was the coolest thing about him.

All of us remember him not as the suave leading man he has become but rather as a jokester who did not take himself seriously. He was incredibly funny. I specifically remember him entertaining us between scenes with impressions, particularly with dead-on impressions of *Back to the Future*'s Christopher Lloyd and Sammy Davis Jr. His Sammy was hilarious—and he could go on forever, turning himself into a lounge version of that coolest of cats.

I found a pretty cool cat myself. His name was—well, never mind his name. He was not famous and probably enjoys his anonymity. He was a courier on the production crew. He was cute and charming. He delivered the scripts to the cast, and when he delivered mine, he always included really sweet, handwritten notes. One night I opened my script and found a missive that said, "Will you go out with me? If so, circle YES and send it back to me."

We kept things hush-hush but didn't hide anything. We had

fun. One night we went for a romantic gondola ride on the canals next to Naples Island in Long Beach.

That turned out to be a good warm-up for a trip I made to Rome to work on the network special *Andy Williams and the NBC Kids: Easter in Rome*. Unfortunately, I did not get to meet Pope John Paul II, as some of the other kids did; my *Facts* schedule prevented me from flying there in time. Still, I spent ten wonderful, amazing days in the city. I pinched myself as I visited the historic sites and museums. As a little girl, I had looked through magazines and dreamed of traveling to Rome, and now I kept saying to myself, "Here I am."

Every corner I rounded seemed to surprise me with a beautiful church, a cheese store, a bakery, or a wonderful tiny boutique or leather shop. Mr. Williams wanted to capture the flavor of Rome, and we shot all over the city: on the streets, in front of the historic sites, and in restaurants and stores.

One day the two of us were shooting a segment in the Ferragamo store, their flagship on the very tony Via Condotti. We were singing a duet. I spotted a pair of chocolate-and-ivory fine leather shoes. They were gorgeous—I mean gorgeous to the point where I gasped the first time I saw them, then pointed them out to one of the young makeup women on the crew, and every few minutes snuck a peek at them from across the store as if they were a hot guy. Except they were shoes. Amazing shoes.

There was also a matching purse. Also amazing. And expensive.

Finally, at the end of the day, I decided to buy the shoes as a present for myself. "It's now or never—and never is going to kill me," I said to myself. And yes, it was a splurge, but I had not indulged in a single thing the entire trip. So I found the manager and told him that I wanted to buy the shoes. He asked which pair. I started to tell him and then decided it would be easier if I showed him.

We were halfway across the store when I noticed the shoes were gone. So was the matching purse that had been next to them. Stunned, I turned to the manager and practically cried. "What? How are they gone?" I had been in the store the entire day. "Someone purchased them," he said. Then he reached under the counter and handed me a box. I opened it and there they were, the shoes *and* the purse I'd admired—along with a card that said, "Enjoy. Andy Williams."

I still have the shoes, the purse, and the memory.

* * *

Then I came back to earth. In early January 1987, I finally started college. It was the spring semester. Since *Facts* still had several more months before the season wrapped, I commuted from our new home in Woodland Hills. But I was finally a college girl.

I enrolled in the general education courses required of all first-year students and loved everything. Buying my books was one of the greatest experiences of my life. I spent hours looking through the student bookstore, holding the reading lists for my courses but unable to resist the distractions of all the other books. I was giddy at the idea that I was going to read these texts and acquire the information on the pages, get it explained in class, and discuss with classmates. This romanticized vibe of new college life was heightened when I thought I had decided on a major—English Lit. Mom looked at me with all the love, patience, and realism in her and said, "What? Kimmy, have something to fall back on. In case you never act again, have a backup plan." No classic movie reference was needed for this life lesson from her. I got it. It's another "Chip Wisdom Nugget" that has stayed with me, guided me all of my life.

About two weeks later, I was walking across the quad, the center area of the campus and the place everyone gathered, when I stopped. A colorful sign for a club caught my eye. Then another sign. There were tables and signs everywhere for clubs and activities. Sororities. Culinary clubs. The Black Student Association. The Physics Club (probably not, but maybe there were some cute boys). Student government. Everything looked fun and interesting.

Everything.

I was thrilled with the sense of opportunity—the opportunity to be in this club or that club, to take this class or that one, to have new experiences, to make new friends...everything. One day, while walking across campus, I was swept up by a wave of joyfulness. I stopped and turned in a circle, trying to take it all in. Suddenly, I realized what I was doing. I was channeling Mary Tyler Moore and throwing my hat into the air.

And I continued to juggle school, the TV series, and my courier boyfriend. I spent so much time on the freeway I felt like I lived out of my sporty Nissan 300ZX—a graduation gift to myself, along with a personalized license plate, GODZKID. I also took a night class once a week to maintain a full load and signed up for several study groups. Active socially, I met students from the UK, Canada, Liberia, and South Africa. I even met the daughter of the president of Botswana.

Emboldened by the college life, I wanted to experiment a little, play things a bit less safe, and have fun. To me, that meant hanging out past 10:00 p.m., occasionally breaking my diet on a weeknight, and maybe meeting someone new (my courier flame and I were not long-term). So when a guy friend of mine invited me to a party at his house, on a Wednesday, instead of saying no thank you, as was my habit, I thought why not have some fun? Except it wasn't that easy for me.

It was 9:00 p.m., and after I changed into clothes more suited to a party than TV with Mom and Lil Sis and headed toward the front door, my mom gave me a look that asked what was up. "I have to go back to campus," I explained.

"Why?" she asked.

"I just need to take care of some stuff," I said. I can't explain why I reverted to childish behavior, but she knew I wasn't telling the truth and it set off her mother-hen alarms.

She put down her book. "I'll drive you."

This was my biggest worry come true. "No thanks," I said. "I got it."

I lost that round. We got into her car and about ten minutes later, when we were about halfway to Malibu, she turned to me and said, "What are you doing?" I stared out the window. "If you're just starting your night now, what are you doing?" I refused to answer until I could no longer take the implication of her question and suddenly I burst through the tense silence.

"I'm not messing around," I said.

"You better not be messing around," my mom said.

"I'm *not* messing around!" I said.

I am painfully aware of how pathetic that story sounds today. My mom and I still laugh about it. All I have to do is say, "I'm not messing around," and it brings back memories and laughter. She will admit to being a little overprotective, but her intentions were good, and I should've simply said I wanted to hang out with friends.

The problem was solved the next semester when I moved into a dorm on campus. My mom and sister cried when I packed up my car and waved goodbye. For the sake of perspective, I was only going about ten miles from home, and I stopped by at least once a week. But it was still a big move. It was also the right thing to do. The TV show *A Different World* debuted that same fall, and though I was not at an all-black college like those characters, they made me want to experience college life to the fullest, and dorm life was perfect for me.

My roommate was a sharp, beautiful girl from Idaho. With jet-black hair and violet eyes, Susan was a dead ringer for Elizabeth Taylor as a young girl. On paper, we did not have much in common. She was a white girl from the Midwest majoring in business, and I was a black girl from Harlem interested in film and TV production. But we were instant friends. We pushed our beds against the window, decorated with posters, set up our desks, and stacked our CDs together. Her parents always addressed care packages to Susan *and* Kim.

One night I decided to get a little crazy and drink an entire strawberry daiquiri. I ended up falling on my bed. "Everything's spinning," I informed Susan, who watched with a bemused detachment.

"Really, Kim?" she said, laughing. "You had one drink. You're ridiculous, such a lightweight."

As the semester went on, I added broadcast journalism to my film and TV production interests. The pace and the skills required appealed to me. Like all the students in the program, I rotated between the different jobs on the school's daily TV news program: anchor, director, cameraman, editor, computer graphics, sports and entertainment reporter, and general assignment news reporter. I profiled Olympic diving great Greg Louganis after meeting him on a special edition of *Hollywood Squares* and interviewed a young basketball hotshot named Michael Jordan.

I was also involved in the religious side of Pepperdine, as were most undergrads there. To me, that is what made the school special. You could be interested in math or psychology, teaching or science; you could be a jock or an acting nerd like me; you could be a dashiki-wearing dude from Liberia studying political science or a girl from Idaho majoring in business; and no matter your background, skin color, or social status, there was a shared interest in faith and living a spiritual life.

It made the large college seem small, friendly, and cozy. If you've experienced something similar, you know what I mean. People's surface differences were transcended and, in fact, celebrated with an appreciative curiosity because of that bigger thing most of us had in common—our love of God. For those who practiced a different faith or none at all, that was fine, too. We discussed our beliefs, asked questions, debated, and learned from each other. As I think about it, I feel like my faith grew even deeper.

I made Religion my minor. I took courses in the religions of the world. I learned about the mechanics of preaching. I took a class on the Bible as literature. Lectures were instructive and provocative, and even a dry, academic approach to religion, as some of the classes took, would be given a profundity by the beautiful campus. Like other students, I walked outside after class and found myself on a mountainside overlooking the ocean. It left no doubt, as far as I was concerned, that God was among us.

You get the picture. I loved school. I was enthusiastic, eager to consume all the knowledge that surrounded me. I knew it was a growth opportunity. My mom had always encouraged me to get an education and use it. Years earlier, she had said, "Make sure you can be in a room and have a conversation about something besides making a TV show. Make sure you can talk about things that are real." I had an older-brother type of friend who underscored that point. He was one of the coolest guys I knew. He dated cool girls and had a point of view and approach to life that impressed me.

One day, we were on campus, sitting out in the sun with our coffees, and talking about various things, from school to our futures. As the conversation wound around to people both of us knew on campus and our social lives, I grew emboldened and opened up about my frustrations with guys. I told him about my history of being put in the friend zone by guys I liked. I didn't only want a social life, I said. I also wanted a love life. I asked him what made a cool girlfriend.

"I think a cool girlfriend is the kind of girl who has things to talk about," he said. "Being able to talk about big things in the world, like history, politics, and social issues, and also about little things, like sports and people—just knowing stuff—that's what makes anyone cool. Like you. You're cool." Then why was I constantly relegated to the friend zone? He smiled and said, "Kim, you're always going a million miles an hour—and I suspect you always have. If you want love to happen, you have to slow down just a little bit to give it a chance to catch up to you."

Hmmm...

Okay. Got it.

8

The Cool Girlfriend

After nine seasons, *The Facts of Life* called it quits. The series was still going strong and anchoring NBC's Saturday night for all the reasons it had remained on the air for nearly a decade. The writers were still addressing controversial issues, the show was still funny, and the cast still had chemistry. In pictures from that final season, we also had hairdos that provide ample proof of why the '80s had to end. We'd taken it to the limit.

Though the network would have renewed the show, Nancy and Mindy wanted to move on, Lisa was engaged, and I was starting my sophomore year of college minus the charming courier boyfriend, who had moved to another show and another part of his life. The stage was set. After more than two hundred episodes and a Who's Who of guest stars—including George Clooney, Jermaine Jackson, Helen Hunt, David Spade, Zsa Zsa Gabor, Charo, Pamela Segall (now Pamela Adlon), Juliette Lewis, Seth Green, and Mayim Bialik—it was time to say goodbye. Following the last taping, the cast and crew partied at a nightclub on Sunset Boulevard. Then, late at night, we drove off into the rest of our lives.

I moved with my roommate, Susan, into a cute two-bedroom apartment near the Pepperdine campus. This was my first real foray into independence, and it suited me. For the first time, I was setting my own schedule. I went to class, studied, got involved with clubs, and explored new interests, like politics. Growing up, my mom had steeped me in the social movements of her youth: civil rights, voting rights, women's rights, the Vietnam War, and so on. When the actor's union went on strike in 1980, she marched in front of the studios with a picket sign in hand—and my tween self marched next to her.

Similarly, she made sure I worked with the Brotherhood Crusade, participated in community parades in Watts and St. Louis, and campaigned for family friend Maxine Waters when she ran for reelection in the California Assembly. I had also testified in front of a congressional committee after a *Facts of Life* episode addressed the sensitive issue of teen suicide.

But the present was what mattered. I was going to be a first-time voter in 1988, and I took that responsibility seriously. I backed Reverend Jesse Jackson. His effort four years earlier had fallen short, but not before introducing a progressive platform (tax cuts on the very rich, universal health care, eliminating mandatory minimum sentences for drug users) that now seems more the norm than the radical agenda of a political outsider.

This time around, I thought he had a shot at the nomination, and being able to vote for a person of color was huge.

I attended several campaign rallies on campuses around the country, and it was at one of the earliest rallies that I met the Reverend's middle son, Jonathan Jackson. Our parents were friends. Mom was a part of Mrs. Jackson's women's delegation to Addis Ababa, Ethiopia. During their layover in London, Mom met Jonathan and Jesse Jr., who were with their father. Mom suggested if Jesse Sr. was going to run again, he should have his sons and me do college compaigning to get the college vote. When he ran again, he called me. After meeting Johnny at the ralley, we talked, had dinner, talked some more, and clicked. Sure, there was a genuine attraction. But we also had politics and a historic sense of purpose, and that was even bigger. We moved fast. Jonathan was three years older than me and a graduate of North Carolina A&T University. He planned on attending business school after taking care of a more pressing matter: getting his father elected president of the United States.

When we were apart, Jonathan sent me beautiful, detailed letters. Like his father, he had a special gift for words and made me feel like I was with him. In a letter from New York, he described gazing across the water at the Statue of Liberty, the campaign, and missing me all in one breath. Was I that girl? Was I really part of this?

I put it down and thought, *Oh my gosh, this is big*.

Jonathan and his brother, Jesse Jr., and I played a key role in getting out the college vote, and as I got involved with Jonathan, I hit the college trail with them. I went out nearly every weekend.

We campaigned very hard throughout Michigan. It felt like I was giving blood. We rode on buses all over the state, trying to stick to schedules and follow an itinerary, yet reacting to moments that felt critical. The spontaneity of charging to a gathering and feeling like we changed hearts and minds, or at least opened them to new possibilities, was a rush.

We were joined there by Rae Lewis-Thornton, a black woman who had been diagnosed with HIV. She was one of the earliest women, if not the first woman, to step into the public eye as a heterosexual woman challenging stereotypes. She had the fire of a genuine agent of change. She evidenced what it took to create awareness and break down barriers so people could live without being swept into the shadows.

The spirit was amazing. I remember arriving in Kalamazoo

on an afternoon when the cold was like nothing I had ever felt before. I had lost my luggage—or it had lost me. I walked into the local campaign headquarters with nothing but the jacket and clothes on my back and the boots on my feet. I bought a toothbrush in a nearby sundry store. One of the girls working the phones there gave me a campaign T-shirt to crash in. I had nothing else with me, none of the items that usually mattered when I traveled, but I did not feel like I needed anything other than coffee and food to fuel me so I could talk to people, hand out fliers, answer phones, and make sure they voted.

Then the Reverend won the Michigan caucus. Suddenly, history seemed possible. Some of the pundits actually thought he might be able to snatch the nomination away from the more traditional Democratic candidates, Michael Dukakis and Walter Mondale. The *Los Angeles Times* ran a front-page photo of the Reverend, Johnny, and myself. I was hoarse from screaming throughout the night as the returns came in. I do not remember any one of us on the inside asking whether America was ready for a black president, not the way people did when Barack Obama ran in 2008. We focused on reaching people of every color, a rainbow coalition, not just black people. However, questions about race, though unspoken, were ever-present: Could the nominee actually be black? Could he come from the south side of Chicago instead of from a famous, powerful family? Could he have a history in the Civil Rights movement? Could he be Jesse Jackson?

For a moment, it seemed like it. Then Dukakis won several important primaries and accumulated enough states to pave the way for the party's nomination, and the moment we worked around the clock to make a reality faded from view. With the Reverend having captured 6.9 million votes and eleven state wins, Jonathan and I went to the Democratic National Convention in Atlanta, hoping that his father might be Dukakis's pick for vice president. We thought that partnership would have a broad and exciting appeal. It did not happen. Dukakis chose old-guard Texas senator Lloyd Bentsen.

I experienced every kind of emotion during that week in Atlanta. In addition to my relationship with Johnny, I attended as an alternate delegate from California. The atmosphere was electric. You can read about politics and primaries and presidential elections, but standing in the middle of a crowded convention floor and listening to speeches from former president Jimmy Carter, emerging superstar Bill Clinton, Texas state treasurer Ann Richards, and '60s antiwar icon George McGovern gave me an exhilarating front-row seat to the unfolding of history.

I cheered till I was hoarse for each of the votes the Reverend did get. Though the outcome was foregone, I still cried at the end when Dukakis was officially named the Democrats' pick. I lost it even more when Jesse Jr. mentioned Jonathan and me in his speech to the convention. All the pent-up emotion drained out of me. When the Reverend took the podium, I had nothing left other than to stand absolutely still, with only my heart beating, so I could hear every word, indeed every syllable, he uttered, as if we were in church on a holy day.

I thought his speech was the most profound of the convention. He talked about the "blood and sweat of the innocent" that led to "his right and privilege" to stand in front of the convention. He acknowledged those who had lost their lives fighting for the right to vote. He addressed farmers, workers, blacks, whites, Hispanics, women, gays and lesbians, and conservatives and progressives. He spoke of health care, housing, and education as a path to hope. He urged people to see their common thread as the only way to progress.

"Progress will not come through boundless liberalism nor static conservatism, but at the critical mass of mutual survival...It takes two wings to fly. Whether you're a hawk or a dove, you're just a bird living in the same environment, in the same world. The Bible teaches that when lions and lambs lie down together, none will be afraid, and there will be peace in the valley...

"The only time that we win is when we come together."
Amen.

* * *

Following the election, Jonathan and I visited each other as often as possible. He flew to Los Angeles, and I traveled to Chicago. I stayed in his parents' home and always got a good feeling from being there. It was the first time I had been included in a large family environment. They were five kids deep and close to their grandparents. I saw the inner workings when they got along, did not get along, drove each other crazy, and ended the day loving each other. They were a normal family, yet they lived with a sense of purpose.

In December, a month after Dukakis lost the election to George H. W. Bush, I was staying with the Jacksons. I was reading my broadcast journalism textbook when the phone rang. Moments later, I overheard Mrs. Jackson and Reverend talking in a hushed, solemn tone. I put my book down and waited. A short time later, they gathered their family and close friends, including me, and shared the sad news that their friend, *ABC World News Tonight* anchor Max Robinson, had died. The Chicago-based newsman was only forty-nine years old.

It was like a sad breath filled the house. The Jacksons knew what their friend had refused to address while he was alive—that he had spent his final days battling AIDS. Upon his passing, though, he requested that his family confirm the rumors as a wake-up to the black community. I watched Reverend transform himself from the private family man to the public figure who would be called upon for statements and to stand larger-than-life ready to lead.

Within these heady times, there were lighter moments. One night Johnny and I went to the movies. During the movie, I laid my head on his shoulder, as cool girlfriends do, but when

I sat up straight again I noticed that one of my braids was still resting on his shoulder. Luckily it was dark and Johnny was engrossed in the movie while I figured out what to do. After my prayer to have it pop back on my head went unanswered, I very slowly and carefully reached up, slid that sucker off his shoulder, and put it in my pocket. "What was that?" he asked.

"Nothing," I said. "Let's watch the movie."

We continued this way for another year or more. We attended events together and went to church as a couple. I had feared our relationship would not survive the post-election reality of our lives. But that was not the case. As we spent more time together, our chemistry, along with our friendship, grew. It was a fairy-tale relationship. Everyone saw that we were good together.

But that wasn't enough. It was early 1990, and we were about two years into our relationship. By taking year-round classes, plus some at night, I had put myself on a fast track to graduation in just three years. As such, the future was right around the corner. I wanted to figure out what I was going to do—and what that would mean for Jonathan and me.

For a while, I thought about broadcast journalism. But I changed my mind after an internship with a local TV news station. Riding along with the station's seasoned reporters as they covered stories gave me a different sense than reading about the process in a book. One time we pulled up at a car wreck that resulted in the death of a local pro football player. Another time we followed the cops to the scene of a drive-by shooting. There, the body had already been removed, but the little girl who had been present as bullets flew was sitting in shock on the curb, the glass of milk she had been holding shattered on the ground by her feet. Around her, neighbors wailed. The reporter I was shadowing surveyed the scene with me and then said, "Okay, let's go ask people how they're feeling."

I put a microphone in front of a woman and asked her to tell me what happened. She shook her head like I was speaking a foreign language or something and said, "No, I can't because I can barely speak right now. People were just shot here. Do you see this little girl? She ain't got no daddy anymore. So get the hell away from me."

This was too real for me. Shaken, I drove to my mom's house and broke down. "I can't do this," I said. "I can't listen to police scanners, waiting for something bad to happen. It's too depressing." I also spilled to Jonathan, who listened and calmed me down. In the midst of his own changes, he had just left an internship with an investment company and was figuring out his own next moves. He wanted to be an entrepreneur. The unpredictability of that bothered me. One time, as I watched him read a book, I wondered if he might ever run for office. I could see him rising up the ranks. I could also see myself with him. As embarrassing as it sounds now, I did let myself wonder, *What if I'm the first black First Lady?*

Then Kim came back to Earth.

* * *

As my senior year at Pepperdine neared, I thought about taking the LSAT. I considered applying to business school at Clark Atlanta. As much as I loved acting, I wanted job security—and security, in general. But the thing was, I loved acting. I had done it almost my entire life, nearly twenty years, and it was not something I wanted to give up, no matter how much I toyed with alternatives. Admitting that to myself caused me to take a sober, realistic look at Jonathan and at us, and at a potential future. I made lists. I prayed. And ultimately I cried.

I cried because I knew where my comfort zone was and where it ended.

I cried because he was an incredible man.

I cried because I loved him.

And I cried because one day I picked up the phone and told him that we needed to talk.

* * *

I had such a difficult time admitting the truth to myself, I couldn't imagine saying it to Jonathan. Nor could he believe what he was hearing after he arrived at my apartment and sat down on the sofa next to me. Yet there I was, breaking up with him. In tears, I explained that as much as I wanted us to go the distance, I was out of my comfort zone when I thought about the future. He was set on pursing his dreams as an entrepreneur, and while I would never ask him to change or compromise for me, I planned to continue to act, which meant we'd both be swinging without a net and that was too much uncertainty for me.

I had no idea whether I was making the right decision. I spoke from a place of love and honesty, and I let Jonathan know that I was terribly conflicted. My head said one thing while my heart said another. All I could do was trust in a higher power and make sure I had lots of Kleenex nearby.

For a long time afterward, I was sad and lonely. At events, someone from our circle inevitably came up to me and asked, "Why did you break Johnny's heart?" Mutual friends like politician Cleo Fields let me know how Jonathan was doing. And then there was Jonathan's incredible father. Several times I crossed paths with Reverend, who stopped, shook his head with mock disappointment, and said, "Oh, you." Then, of course, I got a smile and a hug.

I really wanted to be the cool girlfriend.

I turned out to be the opposite, I suppose. Or maybe not. I was myself and that was all I could be, and really, looking back, it was the best I could be.

But I was barely twenty years old. What did I know? I still had my whole life to figure out.

9

Experimental

One day early in my senior year, I walked into Pepperdine's television studio and got an idea. Thanks to my major in TV and film production, I had access to all the tools needed to make a TV show: cameras, lights, microphones, and free student labor. Pausing by a monitor, I saw the equipment nearby and thought, *What can I do with all that? What about a talk show?*

The idea made sense. Whenever I've had a problem or felt lost, I have received the same advice: go talk to people. See what they have to say. So I wrote a treatment for a talk show called *Campus Spotlight*, pitched my professor, and soon was putting together a crew and organizing production meetings. The best part? I got permission to shoot the talk show in the Smothers Theatre. Even better was the distraction. For me, there's no better medicine for a broken heart than work.

With talented classmates (like my friend Mark Durel) helping me produce the show, we designed a set with two large, purple futon chairs and a backdrop with large letters that spelled KIM. It looked great. We also put together a band that included our fellow classmate Montell Jordan as the vocalist and my friend Darryl M. Bell, who was fresh off his TV series *A Different World*, as the bandleader. Seeing everything come together made me feel like I could stitch myself back together, too.

Then there was the matter of guests. To book the show, I opened my personal address book. Blair Underwood was the first person I called, and the first to say yes. Jason Bateman said he was in, too. At an NBC party, I had introduced myself to Betty White, who was a Golden Girl at the time. I reached out to her team and asked if she would be a guest. "Let me know where and when," she told them to tell me. Gladys Knight said the same thing. Boxing champion Sugar Ray Leonard also came on—which was super big: it was the day after he fought Roberto Durán in Las Vegas. "I don't do any media right after a fight," he said. "But I'm doing this for you, Kim."

Even family friend and surrogate uncle, the late and wonderful E. J. Jackson, a pillar of charitable good work in the community, offered his limousine service. For free! And so it went. It seemed like there was a group of people out there, some who I knew, others who I reached out to for the first time, but they saw me and thought, "Baby girl is grown up. She's in college now. We're going to support her."

My favorite "get" was Whoopi Goldberg. One day I was driving through Malibu Canyon and saw Whoopi driving behind me in her black Jeep. I thought, *I gotta get her on the show*. It was late afternoon, and traffic was backed up. I kept staring at her through my rearview mirror, wondering how I could make contact with her. I considered stopping abruptly and causing her to crash into me. Another, less desperate option was to hop out of my car and run back to hers if traffic backed up badly enough, which it didn't. Then, just before the freeway on-ramp, she pulled into the gas station. *Hallelujah*, I thought.

I whipped around the corner and pulled up to the pump next to her. "Oh my gosh, hi, it's me, Kim Fields. God, I can't believe you're right here. I always wanted to meet you. What a coincidence!" *Blah-blah-blah*. I was nervous. The friendliness poured out of me. Luckily her Jeep needed a lot of gas. And before she pulled away, I had a yes—and her phone number. I was blown away.

The show was a hit on campus. Taping days filled the Smothers Theatre with hundreds of students who enjoyed being able to see these stars up close and listen to intimate conversations. I prided myself on having a unique angle. Having been in the business and in the media since early childhood, I wanted to ask questions I'd never been asked and have conversations that interested me. I focused on growing up, schooling, values, identifying and exploring passions, discovery of self, and lessons learned. No one benefited more than me. I found a voice in front of an audience, and in a way, I found myself.

Not that I was ever lost. But post-breakup, I was sad, confused, and wondering where my decision to split with Jonathan was going to lead. I had spent nearly two years going in one direction. Then I slammed on the brakes and veered left and found myself at the end of a cul-de-sac. The show proved therapeutic. It gave me direction and confidence. And a voice. I got to ask the questions I needed to ask myself. I also got answers, guidance, and wisdom. And I began to feel empowered and excited about the future.

"I can do this," I told myself. "Whatever *this* is going to be."

* * *

I celebrated my twenty-first birthday at a Santa Monica club with a mix of college and show business friends, including the guys from New Edition. A few glasses of champagne led to several uninhibited whirls across the dance floor and into what seemed the next phase of my life. My birthday was followed by graduation from Pepperdine, which was memorialized. A picture of me in my cap and gown, cheering amongst my classmates was *Jet* magazine's Photo of the Week, which made me feel as if all of black America were proud of their baby girl.

Following school, I moved into an apartment with my friend Theresa in Studio City.

Starting in June 1990, I took advantage of not having any commitments for the first time since I began to work at age seven. My schedule was mine, and luckily I was an energetic self-starter. I took a writing course at the American Film Institute. I produced a children's gospel album with mom and our family friend Carvin Winans. I auditioned for TV shows. And at the end of the year, I hit the road in the national touring company of the play *One Monkey Don't Stop No Show*.

We opened in Detroit, and the daily routine put me in my comfort zone. Nightly applause did not hurt, either. After one performance, I received a note from a gentleman wanting to come backstage and meet me. Security checked him out and gave me a thumbs-up. He turned out to be a professional football player with the Lions. He had seen the play with his family. We talked for a while, and then he called me later that night and we talked into the wee hours.

He was smart, sophisticated, handsome, a professional athlete, and a little bit of a bad boy, so the attraction was obvious. What really surprised me was the strong connection we seemed to have from the get-go. From that first conversation, it seemed like we'd never run out of things to say to each other. He sent flowers to my hotel room often and visited when we opened in Chicago. This was on top of more flowers, notes, and late-night phone calls when I got back to my room from the theater. I was smitten.

The relationship burned hot and heavy into spring as the play moved to Houston and Baltimore. Somewhere in that time period, he purchased his first home in a Michigan suburb. It fronted a lake and was gorgeous. He referred to it as "our home" and made comments like, "I'm buying it for us." All my romantic fantasies seemed to be coming true. Then, on the eve of a visit he was making to see me in Baltimore, where the play had received its best reviews yet, he canceled his visit. He said the house was having some work done and he had to be there.

Well, there's work and then there's *work*. After the next night's show, I called him, as was our routine. We spoke every night after I got back to the hotel. It was about eleven-thirty, but instead of hearing his deep, familiar voice, I heard a woman answer his phone. I was stunned. I knew his sister, and it was not her voice. "Can I talk to him, please?" I said. And this chick said, "Well, he isn't available."

"Oh?" I said. "You tell him it's his girlfriend. Who is this?"

There was silence. Then, "Well, he's not available."

I waited. I heard people whispering in the background. Finally, he got on and I went off. "Who is that?" I said. "What is happening? What are you doing?"

He said, "I don't need to explain this to you."

I said, "What? Who is that in my house—since you have always said that's our house?"

He said, "Well, this is just what I'm doing right now."

I felt light-headed. "What?"

He said, "I knew the work it would take to keep you, and I don't want to do that work."

Normally very cool and collected, even in heated moments, I turned into a stick of dynamite with a fuse that quickly burned to the end. "Knew the work?" I said, before slamming the receiver onto the phone. I was angrier than I had ever been in my life. Like David Banner turning into the Incredible Hulk, I whipped around, reared my fist back, and punched it clean through the door of my hotel bedroom. Then I ran downstairs, out of the hotel, and into the night.

It was raining, and the Baltimore harbor was beautiful, so pathetically beautiful. Lights shimmered, boats bobbed in the water, and I walked across the pavement, sobbing until I could not tell my tears from the rain. It was out of every movie where the leading lady gets her heart broken and she runs outside into the rain, crying. I was so crushed. I mean gorilla crushed.

This was one of those moments when I looked up and wondered how God could have left me like this.

As it turned out, He hadn't.

10

An Indie Spirit

I finished the tour. The performances that I thought I couldn't get through when I was overwrought with emotion following the end of my love affair turned out to be the best therapy. I thrived on the routine and of course the applause. Whoever said the show must go on must have been part psychologist. Then there was more healing when I returned home.

It was spring 1992, and the city was in flames from rioting after four Los Angeles police officers were acquitted in the beating of Rodney King. After the smoke cleared, Bishop Charles Blake, the pastor of my beloved West Angeles Church, organized teams of people to start the cleanup process. I was deployed to a shopping center whose stores had been broken into and looted. It was a shock. My mom once had a performing arts school there. We spent several days cleaning and painting stores.

If there is a recipe for fixing the problems we all face, large and small, it has to start as we did there in South-Central LA, with people coming together, connecting, and helping each other get back up. As we worked, I could feel myself rising from the ashes, too. On a social level, we could only take on this one little corner, but in a personal sense, I was reenergized and after a few more months, I knew what I wanted to do next: make independent films.

I had gone to the movies with friends to see John Singleton's riveting debut *Boyz n the Hood*. A few weeks later, I saw Spike Lee's *Jungle Fever*. Then I saw Mario Van Peebles in *New Jack City*. All were inspired movies, and I felt like I had gone to school to do work like this, too. I had ideas and connections, but it was hard to get projects properly backed. I was constantly frustrated. I would live and breathe an idea and then see it stall for no apparent reason. That's the arts for you.

Eventually I found a home at Kolbeco Productions, a small production company run by two friends, Mark Kolby and Rob Johnson. They produced live shows, commercials, and music videos. Malcolm-Jamal Warner directed a rap video for them. After they took me in, I directed a video for gospel singer Vickie Winans and worked on several others for young artists. The Hughes Brothers also did a couple things for them.

Their office had a cool, positive, and creative vibe. Lots of creative people came in for meetings or to hang out. I liked having a place to go where I could meet with writers, talk about ideas, and collaborate. Like everyone else, I knew that I had to keep throwing paint on the canvas if I wanted to be an artist. One day my roommate's boyfriend, Marty, who was also part of the Kolbeco group, recommended meeting a friend of his. "David Green," he said. "You guys should get together. He's a writer and he wants to get his stuff out."

Days later, David and I met for the first of several times and hit it off creatively. He had recently moved to Los Angeles from Houston. He was smart, passionate about film, and focused on a career. One afternoon he got ahold of me and said he knew of an independent film festival that coming weekend in Westwood, near the UCLA campus, and thought we should check it out. The films looked good, he said, and there would be people to meet. I said sure, and then, as always, we talked about ideas.

That weekend, David picked me up. It was drizzling when his black Mazda pulled up in front of my apartment building. I walked out the lobby doors and toward the street as if I were slow-stepping down a Fashion Week catwalk. Though David and I were strictly friends, I still wanted to show off my outfit—a fitted blazer over a black bodysuit. The fact that I—someone who'd struggled with weight and body image—would wear a bodysuit was an event, and David picked up on that. "Hey, look at you!" he said approvingly.

I laughed. "Sir, you are gazing at a SlimFast success story."

With that, I told him the long story of how I came to fit into that outfit, starting with when I was in college and put on the proverbial freshman fifteen. I added to those fifteen pounds my sophomore year. I was miserable. I tried Jenny Craig, Weight Watchers, and other weight-loss programs. I was on one of those restrictive programs when I went to an event with my friend Blair Underwood.

It was a dress-up occasion in a fancy hotel ballroom. Dinner was served and my diet allowed me four ounces of protein, vegetables, and a roll if I had not eaten any bread earlier in the day—which I hadn't. In fact, I hadn't eaten anything all day. I wanted to be able to eat at the event, especially bread. As soon as the waiter brought my roll, I cut it into dozens of little pieces, the better to savor every bite, every morsel of guilt-filled gluten on my tongue.

Midway through the meal, I went to the bathroom and when I came back to the table my roll was gone. I saw the waiter walking away with my bread plate. "He took my roll?" I said in a panicked voice. "Where's my roll?" It was an odd reaction, an overreaction one could say, and Blair looked at me accordingly.

"You want another one?" he asked calmly. I was on my feet, hands on my hips, shaking my head. "No, I can't eat a whole other one," I said. "I rationed that one out."

Blair was confused. "What?"

"Never mind," I said.

My roll was gone; my dinner was ruined. The saving grace was that I was hanging with Blair.

Not too long after that event, I tried the SlimFast diet. Word got back to the company, and I signed an endorsement deal with them and made a commercial. I was even asked to be one of the girls in a calendar for a black student organization on campus. In the photo, I wore cutoff shorts and a short-sleeved, denim-collared shirt and leaned against a shiny sports car. It was glorious because I did not think of myself as one of those sexy calendar girls.

"And here I am in this bodysuit," I said to David, finishing my story. "Continuing to enjoy the low-cal fruits of my SlimFast success."

* * *

We kept up our happy, get-to-know-each-other chatter as David pulled away from my building and started us toward the film festival. It was drizzling again. He turned onto Sepulveda Boulevard, heading south. We went up the hill and through the tunnel where the San Diego Freeway was on our left and the Skirball Cultural Center was on our right. The road was under construction; several areas of the pavement were covered with giant metal plates that made the ride bumpy. It did not seem to matter; between the rain and the traffic, no one was going fast.

I liked the CD David was playing on the radio. "Who is this?" I asked. He nodded toward the CD cover, which I picked up. "Seal? Huh, I've never heard of him before," I said. David stared straight ahead, paying full attention to the road as he talked to me, and never once, not even for a millisecond, did the expression on his face register that something awful was about to happen.

* * *

It was literally a blackout, like I lost consciousness, which I probably did, and when I woke up, we were facing the opposite direction. The car had done a complete one-eighty. The windshield was shattered and I was covered in glass. I still had my seat belt on. I looked over at David. His eyes were closed. I saw a little trickle of blood coming out of the right side of his mouth, the side closest to me. I do not remember if I realized I was all right. Instinct just took over. I realized we had been in a car crash, a very bad one. I undid my seat belt, slowly got out of the car, and saw cars stopped around us, and screamed, "Help us! Help us! Help us!"

I noticed the rain had stopped. Traffic was at a standstill as I wandered in the street.

Why wasn't anyone coming to our aid? To David's aid? He was hurt.

"Please!" I screamed again. "Somebody help."

Just then I felt a hand on my back and heard a woman's voice say, "Just praise Him."

What? I was in shock.

"Just praise Him," she said again while gently guiding me out of the street. She led me to the curb on the opposite side of the street and sat me down. She continued to rub my back, trying to calm me. "Just praise Him." I never turned around to see her. I never saw that wonderful woman, that wonder of a woman.

Two ambulances rolled up. I was placed on a metal stretcher, with my head secured in case I had suffered a neck or spinal injury, and placed in the back of an ambulance. I wanted to say thank you to the woman who had helped me. I looked for her as best I could, but didn't know who I was looking for. I do not even know if she really existed. I believe she did/does. As the ambulance drove off, the EMTs began working on me. One of them started to cut my catsuit. "Hey, wait a minute," I said. "Why are you cutting my catsuit? Do you know how hard I worked to get in this outfit?" As I said, I was in shock; they ignored me and continued to do their job.

As I entered the hospital, I was conscious, but I had disappeared into a semi-there cocoon of shock and stillness until someone asked if there was anyone I wanted them to call. I snapped to. I thought of my mom, obviously, but there was no way I wanted her to experience the shock of a stranger from a hospital calling and saying her daughter had been in a car accident, even if my injuries were minor. I told them to call a family friend, Louis, the man who had chauffeured me and Loy to his senior prom in high school.

Louis was like a big brother, and I knew if anybody could say to my mom, "Kim's been in a car accident," he was the one. He made the call, and soon both of them were on their way to the hospital.

In the meantime, a doctor came into my room to address the difficulties I was having breathing due to what turned out to be a bruised sternum. He also checked the swelling and pain in my arm, due to a severely sprained wrist. I recognized him immediately; his girlfriend was my neighbor in my apartment building. I saw him all the time. "You're okay," he said reassuringly.

My eyes filled with tears. "Are You putting angels around me right now?" I said to God. "Of all the people. Of all the places. Of all the timing."

After he asked a few questions, I asked one of him, the one I dreaded. "How's my friend? How's David?" He took a deep breath before offering me a slight, solemn shake of his head. "He didn't make it." David had died from internal bleeding and injuries he sustained from the steering wheel slamming into his torso. Apparently he was breathing upon arrival at the hospital. But he passed a short time after.

I screamed—a long, guttural, pain-filled, primal scream like I had never heard come out of me before. Then I broke down into a hard, sobbing cry. The doctor held my hand as my cries were occasionally punctuated by more screams.

When my mom came into the room, I suddenly cried even harder. Wordlessly, she took my hand and held it tight. She had heard the news and helped me by being there. Just by holding my hand the way a mother does with her child, being present, and letting her strong heart beat for mine.

I stayed in the hospital overnight. Before I went home, doctors warned that I might experience post-traumatic shock and suggested that I see a therapist. I took names, but returned to my life without any serious side effects. Though I didn't cry, I thought about David constantly. I replayed the accident as best I could. I thought of him picking me up and the way we talked. I could hear him telling me about Seal. And then everything stopped.

This tragedy was profound on so many levels, and I felt like the tears I didn't cry were replaced by questions, starting with the obvious—why David and not me? I thought about it constantly and concluded there probably wasn't an answer, not one that was within my grasp anyway. The randomness of life was impossible to fully understand. It underscored the mystery of life. Why was I born to my mother? Why was I a Christian instead of a Hindu? Why was I an actor rather than a mathematician? Why was I still alive and my friend dead?

For one reason or another, everyone asks these questions. Most are not easily if at all answerable. I decided David left us gifts, including the opportunity to reflect on the meaning of life. What was the meaning of his? What was the meaning of mine? I knew the answer. Life had to be lived with purpose, gratitude, kindness, and love—the love of each other and love for God, who loved us back so we could live.

* * *

My twenty-second birthday arrived soon after the accident. My mom and aunt had a small get-together for me at my Aunt Pat's apartment. Guests included my roommate, Theresa, and her boyfriend, Marty, who had introduced me to David; my friend Marlo Underwood, Blair's sister; and several others. It was very small, and it seemed less of a birthday party than an effort to lift my spirits, though I was not down or despondent as much as I was walking in neutral.

Marlo helped take care of me. I was sore to my bones and stiff, and unsure on my feet. Seeing this close up, she stayed with me for days and helped me move around and care for myself using the bathroom and the shower. It was a whole different level of friendship. It was really sisterhood. I was incredibly grateful but not surprised, in that her parents, Mr. and Mrs. Underwood, had raised their children to be individuals whose actions and deeds reflected such values.

David's funeral was held in Houston, his hometown. I said that I wanted to go. Most everyone around me thought that was a bad idea. They said I was too shaky physically and emotionally. My mother said she would not stop me if the doctor cleared me for travel, but I could tell she was concerned. But those fears were allayed when Marlo offered to accompany me. "I know it will make Mama Chip feel better," she said, before adding to me, "And I know you can use the help."

We flew to Houston and met up with what I called my Houston family—tennis great Zina Garrison; her dear friend, sports reporter Kim Davis; Zina's coach, tennis pro Katrina Adams, who would go on to become the first black USTA president; and others from their circle. After another low-key birthday party with all of them, I got myself together for the funeral. Marlo stuck close to my side throughout the service. Then David's mom wanted me to travel with her and her husband to the burial site, and of course I got in the car with them. David was their only son, the prince of their family, and they were devastated.

Standing beside the gravesite, I was overwhelmed with guilt. As David's casket was lowered into the ground, I wept uncontrollably, the way I had in the hospital. All the emotions I had been carrying around came out. I was staring at the ground and asking, "Why wasn't it me?" when David's mother wrapped her arm around me and drew me toward her. "Please don't say that," she said. "Don't say that. You were the last person to be with my son. You are somebody's child. You are still here. You can't wonder why that is. It just is. You have to live your life."

I could not fathom how this woman who was burying her son was able to summon the strength to comfort me. But she did. I held on to her and let myself cry, as everyone there did, until the well ran dry again. I know her words were what finally helped me begin the climb out of the lingering fog of that tragedy, and perhaps, in a way, we helped each other.

The flight back to Los Angeles continued the catharsis. Something about gazing out the window at thirty-five thousand feet and looking down on the clouds with nothing but blue sky above let me say a final goodbye. Watching the casket get lowered into the ground was one thing, but I had the feeling I was closer to my friend up in the sky, closer to heaven, where my awareness in my faith and in my spirit allowed me to stop asking questions and instead settle back in my seat, close my eyes, and feel the comforting power of God's hand.

Years later someone asked why that incident seemed to strengthen my faith instead of shattering it. I responded by saying I could not have imagined getting through it otherwise. It was my faith that enabled me to stop trying to make sense of a terrible, inexplicable tragedy and move on. While people often have good, logical, and personal reasons to break with a particular church, God is either in your life or not, and if He is, He is omnipresent and omnipotent.

Up in the air, on the way back to Los Angeles, I realized David's grieving mom had told me the same thing. "You have to live your life." Ruminating on those words, I stared out the window at the clouds and the sky and thought back to that feeling I first experienced at the Ward AME Church, back to the warmth of feeling safe, protected, and loved. I needed to get there. I would get there. No matter how hard it got or how alone I felt, He was there with me.

That is faith. He is always there.

God lights the way.

God is all-knowing.

God is love.

11

Regine

It was 1993, and I was in the second week of rehearsals for my friend Tommy Ford's play *South of Where We Live.* I was in jeans and a T-shirt. My stage costume, a casual dress of mine, was on a hanger behind the door. As I began to apply my makeup, a young girl—someone's daughter, I supposed—looked at me through my open dressing room door. Seated in front of a makeup mirror in this small South-Central theater, I had a sense of déjà vu.

I flashed back to myself as a child, watching my mom and the other actors get ready for *Hello, Dolly!* and saw that I had gone back to the beginning, my roots, unconsciously returning to where I was most comfortable and needed to be. It was my way of processing something horrible, healing, and moving forward.

Following David's funeral, I directed several music videos and worked on various ideas, but acting jobs were what I wanted and they were scarce. I did not understand why. I read for *Poetic Justice*, and while I was happy to be considered and get in front of John Singleton, who was red-hot coming off *Boyz n the Hood*, I was frustrated when I got the script and saw the role they wanted me to read for was clearly written for Regina King. I heard her voice on the page; it was perfect for her, and she turned out to be superb. Why bring me in?

Afterward, John asked me to stay and read for the part of Justice. I was given time to study the sides and then did my best. Apparently, John and his team liked me. But the role eventually went to Janet Jackson. It was, I suppose, poetic justice. I got the Mrs. Butterworth's commercial, and she got the movie.

I had a similar experience reading for Keenen Ivory Wayans's movie *A Low Down Dirty Shame*. I auditioned for Peaches, the female lead that Jada Pinkett Smith ended up so wonderfully playing. Rejection is one of the realities of acting—and in any type of job. In order to advance, you have to put yourself out there, and that means risking disappointment. I understood the deal. I had a thick skin. Still, it was hard and hurtful. I had to remind myself that I had chosen this profession.

Back when I was dating Jonathan Jackson, I would sometimes muse about the uncertainty of my career and the lack of job security. He would say, "But you're Kim Fields. You're Tootie. Everyone knows you." Yes, and while I did enjoy a degree of recognition, it could also work against me because I was Kim Fields and everyone did know me as Tootie. Imagine the best part of your life also being a detriment.

There were more challenges. I was a woman—and a black one, two facts of my life that made roles scarce and scarcer. After auditioning for a coming-of-age comedy that I discovered had an all-white ensemble—they'd seen me as a favor to my agent—I called a friend and vented. "Where are the black folks in these pieces? You got *The Breakfast Club*. You got *St. Elmo's Fire*. Where are the black stories? This is why I want to make movies. This is why I want to produce. We've got stories to tell, too."

Guest-starring parts on *Martin*, *Roc*, and *The Fresh Prince of Bel-Air* kept me on the map, but it was *Martin* costar Tommy Ford who gave me a much-needed boost of confidence when he asked me to be in a play he was directing called *South of Where We Live*. It was about young African American professionals at a one-day workshop who confront social issues they thought they escaped after moving from their old neighborhoods. The cast featured Wendy Raquel Robinson, Michael Beach, Pat Belcher, Gigi Bolden, Tommy—and me. I played a sophisticated, sexy woman who seemed superficial but was much more complex beneath the surface.

We performed in front of the hometown audiences that inspired the story at the Ebony Showcase Theater, which had been founded by *Amos 'n' Andy*'s African American actor Nick Stewart. No one got paid. We did it for the love of acting and theater. I was thrilled to have such a layered role to explore. It was a welcome change from sitcom punchlines. At the same time, no one was more surprised that Tommy thought I could handle it than me. "You've got so much in you," he said. "You don't even know it. You don't know how deep you go—but I've got a sense."

Inspired by the play and encouraged by Tommy, I set out to create my next TV series. I wanted to play a grown-up and was sketching out a black version of *The Mary Tyler Moore Show*—a young black girl trying to make it on her own—when I came up with another idea, *Love Byrds*, a weekly half-hour show about a newly married couple whose last name was Byrd, inspired by *Mad About You*, the NBC comedy. I took it to Rocky Carroll, who was red-hot as Charles Dutton's younger brother on the new FOX series *Roc*. I knew him through my sister, Alexis, who was also on the show and was spectacular!

Rocky loved the idea, but he was tied up with *Roc*. He also said my treatment still needed more work to get to the place where a network would seriously consider it. My agent advised partnering with a network-approved writer, someone who could create and actually run a show based on my idea. I knew he was right. I phoned contacts and asked who was great. I kept hearing one name come up—Yvette Lee.

She was described as a really terrific, super gifted writer. She had cut her teeth on *A Different World* and was working on *Hangin' with Mr. Cooper*. Mom, who happened to be working on *Hangin' with Mr. Cooper* as a consultant, coaching Mark Curry, knew Yvette and arranged for us to talk.

The call started out well enough. She thought my idea was an interesting take. I felt good the several times I made her laugh. I looked for little clues that she might say yes. However, when I asked point-blank if she would help develop the show, she declined. She was already committed. "I'm working on a project right now for FOX," she said. "I've got Queen Latifah and Kim Coles attached."

Figuring we were finished, I started to thank her for taking the time to hear my pitch when she hit me with, "There's a role in this show I just mentioned that I can hear you doing," she said. "Actually, as I think about it, I kind of had you in mind for it as I was writing her. She's a bit of a diva from the hood."

I wanted to hear more. "The show is called *My Girls*," she continued, explaining it was about the lives and loves of six twentysomething African American friends in Brooklyn. "FOX and Warner Brothers are doing it. I just finished the script. Latifah and Kim are attached, but the other two girlfriends have not been cast. We haven't started that process. I'd love to tell the studio and the network that we spoke."

"Please do," I said, and from then on everything moved quickly. I received the material and a date to meet with the show's producers. After I read, I saw smiles and nods from all the executives in front of me, starting with Yvette. "Yup, that is exactly what I heard," she said. "You're Regine."

* * *

Soon after my meeting, Yvette arranged for Queen Latifah, Kim, and I to get together at a restaurant in Marina del Rey. We had fun and conversation was super spirited. From the moment Queen Latifah made sure we knew she was most comfortable being called by her real name, Dana, it was obvious we had chemistry. From the get-go, I think we all sensed something good was going to happen.

Then the great Erika Alexander was cast and the show had its four female leads and the indisputable magic that you hope for because it can't be faked. Dana and Kim played cousins/roommates in a Brooklyn brownstone. Erika and I were frenemies. Yvette also added two fantastic guys, T.C. Carson and John Henton, as friends from college who lived in the second apartment in the Brooklyn brownstone.

I liked the statement Yvette and the show itself was making about the portrayal of African Americans: the characters were hip, college-educated, ambitious young professionals, and included a magazine publisher-editor (Dana), an aspiring actress (Kim), a strongly feminist attorney (Erika), a stockbroker (T.C.), a handyman (John), and a fashionista (my character) obsessed with finding a rich husband.

Yvette was the catalyst. Thoughtful, strong-willed, brilliant, and lightning fast with a good line, she'd worked her way up the ranks, understood the process, and conveyed her vision in such a way that we all wanted to get in line and deliver. Then there was Dana. As Queen Latifah, she was the rap star who exuded a charisma and strength that was like a superpower. I could see how she rose up in the male-dominated music world. She was also warm and down-to-earth, and her sense of humor was one in a million.

Kim Coles was hilarious. I was a major fan of her work from *In Living Color* and I started to laugh as soon as she began telling stories. I admired whoever at FOX had approved putting Dana and Kim together in a show. It was inspired casting. As was the very witty, irreverent, and clever Erika Alexander. She intrigued me, and as we spent more time together, I figured out why. She was incredibly comfortable in her skin, and that, as with the others, was positive energy I wanted to be around.

As for the guys, I knew of T.C. Carson from his most recent movie, *Living Large*, and once I met him in person, I was impressed. He had style. He could sing. He was funny. He had a presence. I knew he was going to play well amid all of the strong female personalities. I felt similarly about John, a seasoned comic and cool brother who was quick and proud to tell you that he was from Cleveland. He made everything funny and let everyone know he was happy to be on the show.

We all were.

* * *

The pilot was terrific right out the gate. It was a pleasure to read a script where the premise and the characters were well defined, fresh, yet familiar starting from page one, episode one. It was also very funny, but with an intelligence. The laughs were built from situations and relationships rather than setups and one-liners. Our table read highlighted the rapport we all had onscreen and off. We shot the pilot on the former *Family Matters* stage on the Sony lot, and I swear it filled with laughter every day we fine-tuned the pilot. I was referred to as the veteran—or the vet—which I accepted as a badge of honor. At twenty-four years old, I had spent half my life on TV, and I knew funny. This show was funny.

But I also loved that the show felt like a new style of storytelling in the sitcom space. The *LA Times* critic gave us mixed reviews, citing both "pearls" and "gross exaggeration," and intimated the show would ride on the coattails of its lead-in, the popular sitcom *Martin*. FOX changed the name to *Living Single* and we debuted on August 29, 1993. Within two months, we had a bigger audience than *Martin* and ratings that made us the network's fourth-most-popular series, behind only *The Simpsons*; *Beverly Hills, 90210*; and *Married…with Children*. All classics.

Then came the backlash—or *blacklash*. In a story criticizing TV for stereotyping black men and women, *Newsweek* magazine cited *Living Single* as an example, pegging the women as wise-cracking man-haters and the men as sex-crazed cartoons. "This comedy…is supposed to be a black 'Designing Women,' but it's got quadruple the sex drive and none of the smarts. Though all the roommates have college degrees and upscale jobs, they behave like man-crazed Fly Girls. The men fare no better." We were outraged. Yvette most of all—and I stood right by her. We all did. "It seems that whenever there's a black show, someone has to get the hairs on the back of their neck all up about something," I told the *LA Times*. "I'm really tired of it. I mean, we have a woman who owns her own magazine. We have a female lawyer; we have a male stockbroker and one who owns his own business. Don't we get brownie points for any of that?"

Yes, we were a show of black actors, with one of the few black showrunners, not to mention one of the few female showrunners, but I also thought—indeed, we all thought—*Living Single* dealt with universal themes and issues with broad appeal to all people, not just African Americans. As it turned out, we were right. Months later, the show was number one among black viewers, but beyond that, as *Entertainment Weekly* declared, it was "an unexpected hit."

* * *

My confidence soared. The material Yvette and the writers created was an actor's dream. It provided a green light to exploration, and I took full advantage. Starting with the pilot, in which Regine is seeing a man who is—yikes—married, and then going forward into the season, I had fun playing a grown-up. I loved the process of discovering Regine, figuring her out, reading between the brilliant lines Yvette and her writing team created, and working to make her real.

She was so different from me. She was viewed as sexy and superficial with deeper issues, none of which were really on my radar. Sexy was not even in the same room as my radar. How could I have known the role I was doing for Tommy Ford in his play only months before, in a tiny theater in LA, would prepare me for Regine? Lesson: Take time to nurture, pour into someone else's vision or dream. Aside from being a blessing to them, you don't know the blessing in it for you.

I also loved the way Yvette peeled away layers of Regine as the season progressed. Regine's insecurities were revealed. She was given texture, like the show itself. No one was one-dimensional.

We took five days to shoot an episode—four days of rehearsal and a full day of shooting the show twice, including one time in front of an audience. This was everything I relished about being an actor, the process of discovery, creation, and transformation. The process of rehearsing and getting to try things day after day. The opportunity to work my butt off with our talented cast and crew. I loved driving to the studio. I felt good every time I pulled up to the gate and the security guard waved me in. I got to do something I loved. I got to work.

I would think of the frustration of not getting the jobs I wanted following my graduation from Pepperdine and fill with gratitude that I was now doing the thing I loved more than anything else. What was the reason life changed? Or did it? One of the things I would learn much later, after I was a parent and able to look back with perspective, was that life is a journey of ups and downs, thrills, disappointments, joys, losses, loves, and surprises. The only constant is the one I already knew and acknowledged when I closed my eyes and felt His love and thanked God for being there with me.

12

Creator

Our cast gelled instantly and relationships bloomed. We hung out after work. We went to movies and shows and traded CDs and mix-tapes. Dana rented a house in LA and had all of us over. T.C. loved to cook and also hosted impromptu dinners. I entertained, too. One night, someone asked, "What would our names be if we were African royalty?" Pretty soon we had silly nicknames. Kim was Princess Kalooky (she was kooky). Erika was Princess Dabooty (she had no butt). I was Princess Child Star (for obvious reasons; when said quickly and with an African accent, it became Princess Chester). John was Prince Yack (he loved cognac). T.C. was Prince Uh-Uh (he was famous for starting many sentences that way). And Dana was Princess I've Had It Up To Here (the girl had attitude when needed).

Older and more independent than when I was on *Facts,* I had more fun with these people than I'd ever had in my life. But they (completely unknowingly) gave me an inferiority complex. When I compared myself to them, I felt boring. John had wild tales from comedy clubs, not to mention he was laugh-out-loud funny. T.C. was ten years older, from Chicago, had majored in architecture, and danced on Broadway. 'Nuf said. Erika and Kim were like these superwomen, and Dana, well, she was Queen Latifah, with three albums, a Grammy, and stories about how busting rhymes got her African American behind from Newark to Hollywood. And my Mrs. Butterworth's story, roller-skating across Eastland Academy and loving the Lord, was supposed to compete with all that?

I was a mix of insecurity and admiration. At one point, I considered asking Dana if I could intern at her production company, Flavor Unit, back east. I also thought about asking Erika if I could hang out with her. She had a strong Philly vibe, she was cool, and I thought maybe I could model some of that coolness. What I really needed was someone to tell me that I was not boring—or make me feel less so.

Enter John Henton. Somewhere during all that social inter-action, my cast mate and I picked up on some off-camera vibes. I don't remember the moment it started; not sure how I let him know there was a vibe. Knowing me, I probably said something along the lines of, "I'm kind of feeling you." I do remember his reaction. He was surprised. "What? You're feeling what?" Then he jokingly, tentatively acknowledged a similar attraction. "I'm feeling something, too. But maybe what I'm feeling is you feel-ing me."

Once that was straightened out, we began hanging out and holding hands. I'm sure people saw us as an unlikely twosome. John did stand-up, smoked cigarettes, and drank cognac. He was older than me, had an edge, and I liked that. I was a collec-tion of soft curves in search of a sharp angle or two. But don't get the wrong idea. I wasn't looking to change or willing to compromise my beliefs, as much as I wanted to grow. In that sense, John was perfect.

Both of us shared a strong work ethic. As a comic, he knew

what it was like to create something from nothing. Putting to-gether a stand-up act was hard work, requiring constant writing and rewriting, and risking failure in front of an audience to get the desired reward—laughter. He was sympathetic when I spoke of my frustrations and was supportive when I shared my dreams of producing and directing. He was in the audience when I directed a local production of the play *Vanities*, and he provided invaluable advice and help when I made a short film called *Silent Bomb*.

As John could attest, anyone who spent time around me knew that making a film was a dream of mine. When I spoke about my heroes, I looked not only at Hollywood's greatest actors but also directors, producers, and studio moguls. I also looked at the young, black filmmakers putting out great work and wanted to play in that arena. I believed in my ability; I just needed a way in. Between John's support and the resources I had through *Living Single*, the timing was right.

Midway through the first season, I came up with *Silent Bomb*, the story of a policewoman who becomes HIV positive from a blood transfusion after being shot while on duty. I made up the story while drawing from a variety of real-life influences, including my activist pal from the Jesse Jackson campaign Rae Lewis, whose dramatic story of living with AIDS acquired from a blood transfusion was revealed in a powerful *Essence* magazine cover story; dear family friend and NBA superstar Magic John-son, who went public with his diagnosis as being HIV positive; and a friend of mine from church, Sunshine, who lost her twin brother to AIDS.

I wrote the script with Sunshine, then begged friends and coworkers for favors. A year before, I'd been a member of the crew on Blair Underwood's short film *The Second Coming* and met some great production folks whom I called upon for my project. We shot it in a few days in and around downtown Los Angeles. Every spare minute after that was spent in the editing bay. So many people lent their time and talent for no remuneration, only the desire to help make my vision a reality. It was a reminder of the benefits of belonging to a community. As a final touch, I dedicated the film to my late friend David Green.

My intention was to get *Silent Bomb* onto the festival circuit and into as many screenings as possible, but I lacked the administrative support to keep up with all the requirements. As is my habit, I envisioned doing more than I had time for. Still, I managed to screen *Silent Bomb* at the Black Filmmaker Foundation at New York City's prestigious Lincoln Center. I also earned Best Director recognition at the Black American Cinema Society Independent Filmmakers Awards in Hollywood. *Silent Bomb* would also receive an endorsement from the Magic Johnson Foundation. At the end of the day, I was very satisfied with the project.

* * *

Later that summer, I undertook one more project—my mom's wedding to Ervin Hurd, a wonderful man she met while coaching Steve Harvey on the series *Me and the Boys*, where he was the technical director. Ervin (whom I call Dad) was laid-back but strong and cool, and I saw that he really loved my mom and likewise, my mom adored him. They knew what they wanted in their lives and when they felt that special connection, they leaned in—something I applaud them for doing.

They worshipped together at a fairly new and small church near Inglewood and courted under the guidance of that church's pastor and his wife, both of whom gave their blessing to Mom's and Dad's relationship. After Dad proposed, I hosted my mom's bridal shower at my new house in Toluca Lake and then got to work planning the fairy-tale wedding she never thought she would have. On August 20, 1994, she and Dad exchanged vows, as Alexis and I, her bridesmaids (along with our new stepsisters, Tyna and Nakeya), looked on with tears in our eyes, enjoying our parents' happiness.

Not long after the wedding, I left my longtime place of worship, West Angeles Church, and joined my parents and sister at their church. It was a difficult decision, considering how long I had gone to West Angeles and how close I was to Bishop Blake, his wife, and their family. He was a commanding and clear preacher. I loved the church and the community work it inspired. I loved the way his teaching was relatable and applicable. His sermons are still etched in my mind and my soul, always guiding me and providing wisdom. But there was one thing missing from West Angeles—my family.

After I joined them, I realized that I liked the idea of being a family at church. I had a "family" at West Angeles, but there was something new and deep that I loved when I sat next to my mom and dad and my sister, when I was able to hold their hand, join them in song, and hear them say amen. I also liked the intimacy of the smaller church. The smaller environment was a nice change. Teaching-wise, I found the new pastor strong and practical, and I agreed when he said you couldn't pick and choose which of God's instructions you wanted to roll with. It was all or nothing—and that's the way I felt. I was all in.

Unfortunately, as I got more involved in the church, my relationship with John Henton suffered. Actually, it changed. We were midway through *Living Single*'s second season and I was growing in my faith. It caused me to look at John in a more serious light. Neither of us were children—I was twenty-five and he was in his early thirties—and I wanted to know where our relationship was going. Soon we were having difficult conversations. "Okay, for real, what are we doing? Is this something that's long-term? Where do you see this?"

As much as I asked John these questions, I was trying to

figure out the answers myself. Late one morning at a coffee shop near my house, John and I had an intense, honest, and extremely difficult conversation. We loved each other without question. However, I had been asking myself if that was enough. Was it enough when one of us wasn't into going to church and the other was committed? I would never push my beliefs on anybody, but I still had to ask, "Are we equally yoked? Are we on a similar page? Are we even in the same book?"

We were and we weren't—and that ended a lovely relationship. As word of our breakup got out, I told people that it was not the result of hard times, only hard decisions. Since we were not fighting or running off to date other people, John and I continued to joke on the set and support each other away from work. We remained good friends, which was a relief.

* * *

I found myself in one of those places where I was ready to move on and more specifically, ready to focus on work rather than a new relationship. I had a slate of projects and ideas. Everything felt fresh and strong. With the platform of the show and the short film on my resume, I thought my time had come. However, none of the projects took off. I worked my butt off, yet every executive had a reason why the pitch wasn't right, and the frustration and disappointment put me in a rut.

Marilyn Monroe said, "Hollywood is a place where they'll pay you a thousand dollars for a kiss and fifty cents for your soul." In other words, it's a tough business. I couldn't see the big picture, only the immediate, and only disappointment. I compared myself to everyone else. No matter who I looked at, they seemed to be having more success, especially my friend Dana, who was starring in the thriller *Set It Off*, launching projects through her own production company, and just being

Queen Latifah. I could only think, *What about me?*

It pains me now to even remember thinking this way. It's like a cancer that takes over positivity and rational thought. Everything becomes, *What about me? Why not me? I'm not jealous, just ready for my harvest.* I had set a timeline for myself. By age thirty-five, I wanted to be living on a ranch with my kids and my husband. I wanted a production company, maybe my own studio, and a church, which I would build in the cute little town near my ranch. It seemed feasible. I was creative, hardworking, and determined. I had the tools. But when it didn't happen, I was like, "What's up, God? Where are you? When is it my turn?"

Being a person of faith and yet feeling like this anyway was the worst part. I knew everybody's blessings were meant for them. I knew all the right things to say—and repeated them till I was deaf to their meaning. I told myself that it was not my season—and then I wondered when it would be my season. I wore T-shirts with proverbs (*Better a patient person than a warrior*). I filled my dressing room with pillows bearing consoling quotations (*At the proper time we will reap a harvest if we do not give up*). I bought inspirational cards (*The Lord will fight for you; you need only to be still*).

I kept up a running conversation with God—in the shower, in my car, between scenes on the set, and as I lay in bed trying to go to sleep. "You said you'd give me the desires of my heart. You said to whom much is given, much is required—and I feel like I'm living up to my requirements." I ran down my resume to Him. "I'm at my church regularly. I'm tithing. I'm helping in the community. I'm studying. I'm giving it to others. I'm pouring it into their visions and dreams. It's not all about me. But I'm ready for some of it to be about me."

Really ready.

And then...

13

Bride

I first noticed Johnathon Franklin Freeman at church. Living in San Diego where he worked in sales and marketing for Calloway Golf, he had friends in LA who worshipped at our church and he joined them whenever he spent the weekend in town. He also took acting classes with my mom in a small theater in Hollywood. He was more of a hobbyist than a want-to-be star.

I liked him. He checked all the boyfriend boxes: handsome, smart, athletic, funny, and charming. I could see why he was good at his job. He fit easily into a small social circle I was part of at church. We were a mix of guys and gals in their twenties who hung out together, and Johnathon drove up from San Diego more and more frequently to fill the empty chair that was usually next to me as the only single member of the group. Before long, we were in a relationship.

Born in Vietnam, Johnathon was a war baby who was adopted by an American family through Catholic Charities. He grew up in Boston and went to college in Florida, where he was a star athlete. After graduation, he went to work at Callaway Golf in San Diego. He was doing well there when we met, but he aspired to starting his own marketing company. Given my aversion to being in a serious relationship with someone who didn't have a safety net, I should have listened to my inner voice as it cautioned, "Take it slow."

But Johnathon's job at Callaway kept me in my comfort zone. And not only did he pass the "Mom Test" at church, but he also passed more of my tests. He seemed focused on his faith and developing his relationship with God. He wanted to grow as a person. "I'm happy for you," John Henton said when I told him that I was in a new relationship. Then he jokingly added, "Now get out of my dressing room."

A few months later, toward the end of the season, Johnathon—what was it with me and guys named John?—surprised me on the set. We were in the midst of taping a show, and I was in one of the quick-change dressing areas behind the sets, putting on a different outfit between scenes, when he said hello, gave me a kiss, and then got down on one knee and presented me with a diamond ring. "Oh my God," I shrieked as I covered my face with my hands, as if to stop my world from spinning out of control. My eyes filled with tears. "Oh my God."

My cast mates and crew watched through the open curtain of my dressing area. Cheers and applause followed. In case those in the control room were wondering why I wasn't back onstage, I grabbed the headset from the stage manager and said, "He proposed! He proposed! He proposed!" Word spread almost instantaneously through my circle of family and friends, and the reaction was joyous. "Sis, you love love," said my friend Mark Kibble of the group Take 6. "You love to care for people. No one deserves to be married more than you."

After setting a date in late July, I began to plan my wedding.

Not that I needed to think about it much. Like nearly every girly girl, I had fantasized for years about my wedding. I had saved bridal magazines up to my eyeballs. I had dog-eared pages and ripped out pictures and organized everything in a file. I even knew exactly where I wanted the party. Back in college, Pepperdine had held a dance inside the Avalon Casino ballroom on Catalina Island, and the grandeur and romantic look of that building had imprinted itself in my head as the place I would celebrate my betrothal, once that special day arrived.

Now, it was written in my planner, the date circled in red and embellished with little hearts. I pictured myself in a first dance, gracefully traversing the world's largest circular ballroom in my gown as our family and friends watched breathlessly, framed by the French doors that circled the room. Flowers everywhere. An orchestra playing on the Romantic Promenade above. And . . .

Well, you get it. If it sounds like I went a little overboard, it is because I did. Hey, that is me. I am a planner, a romantic, a dreamer, and, in terms of my vision of a wedding on Catalina Island, I'm also a water baby. I love the water—being on it, in it, looking at it, watching the waves, staring off into the distance, and seeing Johnathon and I exchanging vows on a vintage, double-masted schooner that sails the wedding party twenty-six miles across the Pacific to Catalina for a gala reception in the 1920s-era Art Deco/Italian Renaissance–style landmark.

Earth to Kim!

Earth to Kim!

Come back to reality!

Wake up!

* * *

Planning the fantasy wedding was interrupted briefly when I helped Brandy prepare to star in her own TV series, *Moesha*. She was friendly with my sister, and the show's producers asked me if I would spend some time with the teenage pop star as she transitioned to acting. Initially, I was reluctant to say yes, knowing I was focused on my wedding and had a short window of down time before *Living Single* started its next season. But Brandy was touring with Boyz II Men. Going on the road with them sounded fun. I heard Brandy was a sweetheart, which proved true, and I was already really good friends with the guys. The previous summer, I'd received a call from a casting director friend during Mom's bridal shower I was hosting at my home. I was offered a role as one of the girlfriends in the upcoming Boyz II Men video, "On Bended Knee." Well let me tell you...Mom and I did our usual celebration. Yes, there in the middle of the shower games and gifts! To be requested by big stars like Nate, Mike, Shawn, and Wanya to be one of their girls in a video? You know the next words: You could have bought me for a penny and asked for change. We filmed the beautiful video in New Orleans. It's still a career highlight and treasured memory, as well as the gateway to friendships with four wonderful and talented gentlemen.

I liked Brandy immediately. We worked on different types of acting exercises before she got ready for her concerts. *Moesha*'s producers sent us outlines and scenes. Brandy was a good student and a hard worker. She had natural comedic instincts. She impressed me by asking all the right questions. Not only did she want to know all the on-camera stuff about doing a TV series, but she also asked me to describe everything that went on behind the scenes. "I want to know as much as you can tell me," she said. "I don't want to be blindsided."

She and the guys in Boyz got a kick out of watching me obsess about my wedding. She was young and the guys were all single, so planning was its own comedy to them. I had hired a wedding planner to help out while I was on the road. But she lasted only a few weeks. No matter how much we talked, she seemed to have her own vision for how "Kim Fields" should get married—not what I wanted but what she wanted. Finally, I said, "Never mind," and took over the planning myself. *You know what?* I thought. *I know how to run a production. This ain't nothing but a production.*

I asked two production assistants from *Living Single* to help, plus an interior designer friend whose work on Blair's home had knocked me out, and I put my team to work. First, we put together my wedding navy. We found an old-fashioned schooner exactly as I had envisioned for the wedding ceremony in Newport Beach and then we secured a ferry to take everyone not in the immediate wedding party to Catalina, where they would watch us exchange vows on oversized TV screens in the ballroom.

Next, we tackled flowers, food, music, and seating arrangements. Everyone who heard me run through the details stared at me in disbelief at the extent of the undertaking. But this was my way when I tackled a project, whether I was directing a TV show or planning a wedding. I was organized, passionate, detail-oriented, and determined. I was like most women: My wedding was a major production. Even the invitations were little boxed treasure chests filled with various RSVP cards.

Then we hit a snag. Johnathon and I had just started premarital counseling at our church when the pastor asked to meet with me privately. I thought he wanted me to answer some personal questions that he could weave into his service when he married us. Instead, the pastor informed me that he wouldn't perform the ceremony and advised me to rethink the marriage altogether. "The decision is ultimately yours," he said. "But as I've come to know both Johnathon and you, I feel like the two of you are not equally yoked."

I was dumbfounded. "Do you mean spiritually we are not in sync?" I asked. "If that's the case, I disagree." No, he said, trying to be delicate, he thought we lived in worlds that were significantly different. "You mean we can't be married because we aren't in the same tax bracket?" I asked. He nodded. Well, I strongly disagreed and left the church—literally.

I ran down the stairs from Pastor's second-floor office and outside, where I got into my topless Jeep and peeled away from the curb in a rage. "Why couldn't there be a middle ground?" I asked. "Why couldn't there be a 'here's some things to watch out for or work on'? Why was it all or nothing?"

I made an all-or-nothing decision of my own. I quit that church. So did Johnathon. We did not step back in there again.

The fallout was heartbreaking. All but one of our dear friends from the church sent word that they either could not or would not attend or be in the wedding. Only actress Cassi Davis, who would go on to be a major star for Tyler Perry, confirmed her plans to be there. She had moved to LA and stayed at my house for about a year, and we had a ride-or-die friendship. "I will still be a member of that church and love my pastor," she said. "But you're my friend. We've been through a lot together. I'm going to be there for you."

My poor mom was torn between her child and her faith, and in one of the hardest decisions she ever had to make, she chose to obey her pastor. That made me more angry at him than ever. How dare he put my friends and especially my own mother in this position! This should have been a special time for the two of us: going to fittings; talking about flowers, food, and place settings; and sharing all the intimate, loving mother-daughter moments that precede a marriage. Instead, I had to look to the other women in my village for hugs and support. It was not an easy time for either of us, but eventually, after many conversations and prayer, my mom came around and decided to attend the wedding.

* * *

On the morning of my wedding, I was preparing to get a massage in my hotel room when the phone rang. I didn't want to answer. T.C. had gifted me with a wedding morning massage from a good friend of his who was a professional masseuse, and he was standing by. When the ringing persisted, I picked up the phone and heard my mom's voice. "Baby?"

I thought, *Oh no, she's changed her mind and decided not to come.* But rather than jump to any conclusions, I took a breath and said, "Yeah?"

"Have you looked outside?" she asked.

"No," I said, before walking across the suite to the windows. I pulled the drapes and saw the sky was filled with dark, gray clouds. It was drizzling, too. My heart sank. It certainly was not the kind of day to sail over to Catalina on an old-fashioned schooner.

"Don't panic," my mom said. "Everything's going to be all right. The rain is here to wash everything away and make all things new."

She was right. By the time the wedding party boarded the schooner and charted a course for Catalina, the rain had stopped and the sky was clear. The ceremony on the schooner was as lovely as I'd imagined. About twenty-five family members and close friends watched as my sister, Alexis; my other amazing sisterfriend bridesmaids Gigi Weatherspoon-Bell, Katrina Adams, Carol Kim, and Andrea McClurkin-Mellini; and my flower girl, Andrea's daughter, Brittany, preceded me down the aisle. Then, while holding a small bouquet of white roses, I stepped carefully, in an off-the-shoulder satin and lace gown designed by my godmother, Victoria Shaffer. Being uber traditional, I even asked my father, Tony, to give me away, with my dad, Ervin, lovingly by Mom's side.

My hair was pulled back into an elegant chignon, and I wore a small hat with an ivory veil. Johnathon had asked me not to wear much makeup, if any, explaining that he thought I was beautiful without it; and indeed, as I took my place beside him,

Johnathon looked at me and whispered, "You are so beautiful." Clarence McClendon, the bishop at our new place of worship, Church of the Harvest, handled the ceremony. It was perfect.

The celebration kicked into high gear once we arrived on Catalina, where another two hundred people, including my *Living Single* and *Facts of Life* cast mates, ate, danced, and partied into the night. At some point, my friend Carol had snuck off and primed the honeymoon suite in a nearby hotel for romance, with rose petals strewn across the bed, a waiting bubble bath, sparkling cider on ice, and soft music. At midnight, when Johnathon asked if I was ready to leave the party, there was no confusion when I took his hand and purred, "Ready."

* * *

For our honeymoon, we flew to Acapulco and promptly got into an argument that, in my opinion, needn't have happened but might have foretold future issues. Consider: As Johnathon knew, I struggled with the idea that I was boring and had been boring my entire life, and now that I was his wife, I was ready to change my MO, so to speak. Where better to start than on your honeymoon?

So while Johnathon was playing golf, I got out my eyeliner pencil and wrote him a special message on the side of the double-soaker spa bathtub: "Meet me in here tonight." That was me getting freaky. Well, he saw it and flipped out. "What if it doesn't come off? What if we have to pay for a new tub?"

That was not the response I'd wanted. "Really?" I said. "Not 'Wow, baby, this is going to be a fun time tonight.' Instead, you're thinking, 'Hopefully this comes off so we don't have to pay for it.'"

After getting past that hurdle, I was sidelined with a sinus infection that spoiled the next couple of nights for both of us. We made the best of the rest of the vacation. He played golf, which was his passion, and I sat in the golf cart with a good book, one of my passions. We hit the beach, went sightseeing, and enjoyed good food.

Back home, Johnathon moved into my San Fernando Valley house and we settled into an everyday routine. I returned to *Living Single* for a third season, while Johnathon, who quit his job with Callaway in order to move to LA, partnered with a friend and launched a branding and licensing company. They customized jackets, T-shirts, coffee mugs, and other items with logos on them. NASCAR was an early client. For Christmas, I hired them to do sweaters with the *Living Single* logo on them and gave them to the cast and crew. The next year, the cast ordered show jackets for the crew.

I also started my own production company, L'il Mogul Productions. I brought in a head of TV, a head of film, and an assistant. We struck up a relationship with the Christian publisher Zondervan to develop books into TV and movie projects as intended and also explored business opportunities in Harlem, which was starting to enjoy a revitalization. Despite my earlier setbacks trying to produce projects, I thought we had the right combination of talent, experience, and ideas to break through.

But Hollywood is a tough, unpredictable, fickle business, and I didn't have to look any farther than my own show. Warner Brothers produced both *Living Single* and NBC's newest hit, *Friends*, and we felt the studio favored the newer and, dare I say, whiter series. The evidence was right in front of us. Billboards for both shows went up outside the studio gates, where we drove in every morning. Ours was a third of the size of *Friends*. "It just pisses me off every time I see that *Friends* billboard," Queen Latifah told the *LA Times*. Our showrunner, Yvette Lee Bowser, spoke for all of us when she said "It's disappointing that we have never gotten that kind of push that *Friends* has had."

Both shows were about six friends dealing with relationships, careers, and trying to figure out life. Except one cast was all black, and the other was all white. "You can't deny the similarities," Yvette said after *Living Single* was moved to Thursday nights, which pitted the two shows against each other. But the dissimilarities were what enraged us. At one point, the cast of *Friends* walked off their set to get more money. By contrast, we staged a protest during season three, refusing to come out of our dressing rooms, in order to get the heat turned up on our soundstage. We were freezing! We rehearsed in big, puffy winter coats. You haven't lived until you have seen Kim Coles do Synclaire in an ankle-length down jacket with a San Francisco 49ers logo on it pulled from a wardrobe closet.

That was one of many incidents. For instance, that same season, we did not get a prep day with the new makeup artist before our new opening title shoot. Our wardrobe was also delivered wrinkled. "You can't just give our costumer the key to the wardrobe trailer and say, 'Go throw something on them; we start filming in twenty minutes,'" I said. We constantly fought for respect. I hated hearing people say, "Well, you're the number one black show." Why was that the bar?

There was a lot going on, in many directions, but I was happy at the end of the day when I was able to go home and spend the evening with my husband. I enjoyed being a wife to Johnathon and one-half of a partnership. Call me old-fashioned, but I cherished those values. As for Johnathon, he got two versions of me: the private and the public, and I'm sure the latter wasn't easy. Whenever we went out, someone invariably stopped me for an autograph or a quick word, and I obliged. I understood fandom. I still had my Rick Springfield Fan Club membership card and a pink sweatshirt from his concert Janet and I went to. But I also understood the deeper human need for connection and the atypical role I occupied in the world. I'd grown up in millions of people's living rooms. They saw me every week. They watched me grow up. They followed me on camera and off. To them, I wasn't a stranger. Even if I was, ain't nothing wrong with a world where strangers practice random acts of kindness.

While nothing takes God by surprise, things were about to jump off that would surely take me by surprise.

14

Frustrated

Church on Sundays affected me in a variety of ways. It fed my soul. It opened my eyes. It warmed my heart. It deepened my relationship with the Lord. It renewed my understanding of His power. It connected me to community. It inspired me. It shaped my week. It recharged my batteries. It reminded me of God's presence in my life. It provided a blueprint for applying His Word to my everyday life. It helped me to deal with the frustrations of running my company. It did so many things.

And on this one Sunday, I heard the bishop say, "Don't let small-minded people lock you down. The Lord strengthens us. Jesus is a healer and a deliverer." This inspired me to ask for help. Not to mention that during one of our regular life chats, Blair had recently (and gently) reminded me, "Kim, you don't like to ask for help. But you could be blocking someone's blessing of helping you . . . Don't be a blessing blocker." After hearing Blair's and the bishop's words—*Jesus is a healer and a deliverer*—I prayed on them, and about two weeks later my agent asked if I wanted a summer job directing the new Nickelodeon series *Kenan & Kel*, a spin-off of the network's hit *All That* starring Kenan Thompson and Kel Mitchell. Was it an answer to my prayers? Or just a coincidence of timing?

I didn't try to figure it out. I expressed my gratitude to God and then asked my agent where I signed. It turned out my work was submitted to the show's executive producer, Brian Robbins, a former teen actor who had appeared years earlier on *Facts of Life* as Natalie's love interest. Brian liked that I knew comedy and what it was like to be a child actor—and a funny one. And I got the job.

They shot over the summer in Florida. It was during *Living Single*'s hiatus, so it was perfect for me. As soon as we wrapped, Johnathon and I decamped to Orlando. They put us up in the Peabody Hotel, a luxury offshoot of the famous hotel in Memphis. For my first episode, I left Johnathon to play golf and visit his family nearby while I drove my rental car along Interstate 4 to Universal Studios, blasting the Eagles' "Hotel California" on the radio. I loved that drive. By the time I parked in front of the Nickelodeon soundstage, I was in the zone. My sleeves were rolled up and I was ready for work.

I directed four episodes that first season and loved every minute, including the commute from LA. I was able to exercise different creative muscles and draw on years of experience. I was comfortable in that world. I also liked the people. Brian and his partner, Michael Tollin, and their buddy, Dan Schneider, another former-teen-actor-turned-writer, were great guys. I felt the same about Kenan and Kel, both of whom were gifted sketch comedy artists and impressive young men.

On the set, I admired their attitude and approach to their work. They did not behave like typical teenagers. They applied themselves to every scene. They knew they were good and wanted to get even better. Off-camera, I was blessed to have many candid conversations with them and the entire cast and crew about life and the importance of developing interests beyond the show to ensure they grew as human beings. I figured I was clicking with the guys when Brian and Michael asked me back the next season.

I looked forward to it. The fourth season of *Living Single* was marked by the ups and downs of a seasoned show where everyone, from the stars to the producers and writers, looked for their next moves. It's the nature of the business to capitalize on success. Our showrunner, Yvette, was developing a new series for the network. I was given the opportunity to direct an episode. Dana was making a movie. John headlined comedy clubs. No one gave less than one hundred percent, but the entire cast expected the show to improve each season, and given how strong we came out of the gate, that kind of high standard was probably unrealistic.

Living Single was good, period. I had to embrace that fact—and maybe that was enough.

On top of that, my marriage was starting to wobble. Now, there are at least two sides to every story about why a relationship goes awry, and I'm sure that's true of mine. More than a year into our marriage, Johnathon discovered that being Kim Fields's husband was not without its challenges. Hey, just being Kim Fields had its challenges. At times, he felt like he was married to all of black Hollywood. Other times, he found a woman wrestling with the insecurities and frustrations that come with working in Hollywood. Then, at night, perhaps, he wanted Regine and instead got a woman who fell into bed in an old T-shirt after working a sixteen-hour day.

That's not to say I didn't get my sexy on. I had a picture of who I wanted to be as a wife, but I didn't always know how to execute. Over time, I'm still learning more of the nuances: how to be sexy, how to be sensual, how to let my husband know that I desire and need him. But that's called experience. Yet, I'm still a work a progress; we all are, if we're honest. We are all always learning about ourselves and each other—under construction.

I guess what I'm trying to say is that Johnathon and I were still getting to know each other, which was complicated because we were still getting to know ourselves. To that end, I took acting classes from Ivana Chubbuck, one of Hollywood's premiere teachers. Her techniques, which were emotionally heavy and raw, pushed me into uncharted waters when it came to examining my emotions, and that bled into other areas. As a result, I started seeing a therapist. I found it beneficial to talk about the way I felt my life, at age twenty-eight, was changing in ways I couldn't always control or understand.

One of the things I worked on in therapy was more acceptance of my body, both the parts I liked and didn't like. I played a woman who was comfortable and confident when it came to her womanly attributes and I worked on adding more Regine in my real-life roles as a woman, a wife, and my husband's lover. To do that, I needed to like my body, to be able to stand in front of a mirror and see it as a positive and to put on clothes—or take them off—and feel at ease and secure. That process led me to a second breast reduction, this time for purely aesthetic reasons.

I had the procedure in the middle of the summer, during a break from directing new episodes of *Kenan and Kel*, and after years of struggling with my body image, I finally felt like I was in proportion from head to toe. Less than ten days later, I was back on the set in Orlando, and not only did I direct that week's episode, but I also acted in it. I played Kenan's substitute English teacher. He thought I had a crush on him. In one sequence, he had a dream in which we did a very funny tango. I forgot my chest was wrapped in bandages and I was on heavy-duty Advil for the next week.

* * *

Like me, Johnathon was trying to figure out what he wanted to do with his life. In addition to his work, he began taking acting classes again. As a former college athlete, he told me he missed the rush of competing in front of a crowd and thought acting might be a good substitute. I supported it as a hobby. But at some point, Johnathon decided to pursue acting full-time, which was his prerogative. But it was a game-changer for me. Though I didn't want to kill his dreams, I had already pledged my support to one career change, and this one was even riskier.

We had many talks, during which I found out Johnathon was also thinking about going to qualifying school and competing on the pro golf circuit. Like so many of us, he was trying to figure out the answers, the moves and paths for his next phase of life. But unlike most people, Johnathon's search was driven by deeper issues stemming from childhood. At age seven, he had been taken from his mother in Vietnam, was put on a plane to America, and was eventually adopted by a family in Boston.

This was in 1975, the same year my mom had auditioned for *Hello, Dolly!* How different our lives were: While I was watching actors prepare for their roles onstage, Johnathon was one of ten thousand babies and small children, some presumably orphans, who were part of a mass evacuation known as Operation Babylift. Obviously not all of the children were orphans, my husband being an example. I imagined Johnathon as a little boy being torn from his mother's arms. I tried to picture that happening to me. It was too horrific.

Yet this was my husband's reality. He'd experienced this nightmare and bore the scars. Now, as a grown-up, he wanted to see if he could find his family, reconnect with his mother, and heal some of those wounds. No wonder he was still trying to figure out who he was and what he wanted to do with his life.

* * *

In the meantime, as *Living Single* went into production of its fifth season, we heard whispers it would be the last one, and gradually word leaked from the network's executive corridors indicating as much. The second episode was T.C.'s last until the finale, and the way that went down—with T.C. seeing the story line, asking if they were getting rid of him, being told no, and then getting told goodbye—underscored that we were ultimately part of a business. Nevertheless, we all felt that he deserved better.

As the season continued, the characters were no longer being serviced by the scripts the way they had been in previous seasons, and while I can't speak for others, the lack of the creative snap and crackle I loved as an actor took a toll on me. Some mornings I had to push myself to drive to the studio. I created exits and entrances for Regine to give the illusion that she still had a fulfilling life to live. In one episode, we were in the woods and a guy pulled a gun on us. I created a "faint" for Regine, so she didn't have to be present for the rest of the scene, which we all felt wasn't our above-par quality. Thankfully the "faint" and the exits fit Regine and were very funny, so I was allowed to keep them.

When it got to the point where, if I wasn't needed, I stayed in my trailer and read a book rather than hang with the cast and crew, I met with my manager and agents and asked them to negotiate an early exit. "I can't do this anymore," I said. "And I don't want to. It's hurting my soul." I couldn't believe those words were coming out of my mouth. Unfortunately, the studio refused to let me go early, reminding my team that I was under contract.

What I really wanted was a production deal, an arrangement that would set up my company, but the studio declined that request, too. They agreed to phase me out with a story line that showed Regine getting the man—and the mansion—of her dreams, and in the end, I was satisfied when I took my final bow. Funny, I remember thinking about how uneventful and thankless the *Facts of Life* ending had been for a show and characters that had so much meaning and success for nearly a decade, yet Regine's sendoff was the stuff dreams are made of for an actor, and all the Regines who do get their prince. I'll always be grateful to Yvette and the writing team for that.

* * *

The stress at work didn't help my marriage, which simultaneously sputtered to its own conclusion. Both Johnathon and I were dealing with personal issues, and looking back, we lacked the maturity and communication skills to work through them together. Marriage is a team effort, and we didn't function like a team. The turning point came when Johnathon went to Vietnam just before Christmas, following new information that he hoped would lead him to his family.

Though I prayed he would find his mother, he was gone for two weeks and during that whole time I never felt like my husband was halfway around the world. I never felt what I would describe as a missing piece in my soul. That's the way it should feel when your partner is away. Instead, I felt more like my roommate was on vacation for a couple weeks. As I recall, this realization caused me to fall on my bed and cry. The truth was sad and painful and set in motion the end.

I spoke to my pastor and my mother, prayed and meditated, and when Johnathon returned home, we spoke about the situation. He apologized and said he didn't realize our relationship had gotten this bad. He suggested counseling, something I had put on the table six months earlier, but I was past that point now and let him know that for me our marriage was done.

Johnathon packed some stuff he had brought upon moving in and took them, along with his bags from his trip to Vietnam, which were still packed, to a friend's house. Seated on the couch, I watched him leave and sat there until the sun faded and the room turned dark, and I literally felt myself become enveloped in a cold silence. It was a sobering moment, a difficult one to accept and not feel like I had failed, but it was real and I gave myself permission to feel this way.

Yes, I recalled that our former pastor had raised a cautionary flag about Johnathon and me getting married, but I was pretty sure our marriage ended for reasons other than those he'd cited. I also thought about the dark clouds and rain that had preceded our wedding day and wondered if I'd missed warning signs. Finally, I told myself that love in your twenties is a crapshoot. I thought I'd found the person for me. I thought I'd been found ("He who finds a wife finds a good thing" and all). I thought I was a good thing. But it worked out differently. Perhaps simultaneous identity challenges personally and professionally for us made the hard work of marriage ten times harder. When all was said and done, I was glad we didn't waste each other's time or hurt each other out of frustration. It was a deeply disappointing ending. Then at some point, I prayed to keep the wisdom but not bring the baggage to whatever and whoever might be in His plan for me. Most days, I subconsciously wondered to Him, *You still got a plan, right?*

* * *

Across town, my *Living Single* family took their final bows without me. My last episode had been a few weeks earlier. It was a bittersweet time, and then, as the weeks passed, it just turned bitter. Here I was, inching toward the latter part of my twenty-ninth year, and when I looked at my life, I thought, *This isn't what I signed on for, not based on the steps I've taken, the prayers I've said, the work I've done, and all the seeds I've planted.* I was no longer on a TV show and didn't have any projects lined up. My production company wasn't producing any fruit. And I was about to be divorced.

Dana once described me as someone who put her life in boxes. Everything was compartmentalized. Relationship in this box. Acting in that box. Body image issues in that one over there. Close the lid on the *Living Single* box. Hers was an accurate observation. She saw me. And at the time I was surrounding myself with boxes. I did not see it, but I was climbing into one of my own.

I was frustrated.

I was fading.

I was . . .

15

Powerful

Iwas stuck in a rut with no idea how to get unstuck, which meant it was going to be a difficult period in my life. And it was. With my marriage over, work strangely absent from my vocabulary, and little desire to do anything or see anyone, I retreated to my bedroom. One day, I went to Home Depot and bought several gallons of gold paint—not the loud gold but a muted, deep jewel gold, and I painted my beautiful white ceiling. A week or so later, I noticed some paint had dripped on the carpet. I picked at it, and then I pulled at it, and soon I was spending my days pulling up the carpet on my bedroom floor. I stopped when there was nothing but raw subfloor. I thought it was artsy. Now I'm like, *What's wrong with you?*

To complete the picture, I put blackout drapes over the windows. Forest green in color, they were thick and heavy. When closed, which was the way I kept them, they kept out the sunlight. My room was a constant shade of midnight, the only light coming from my television, which I watched from my large four-poster bed, a glorious, cushiony island of solitude from the Bombay Company. I loved it—no doubt a little too much for my own good.

I spent every day there.

Alone.

In the dark.

You do not need to be a therapist to understand the situation. On the cusp of turning thirty years old, I was a confused, pained, frustrated young woman. I was unsure of my footing; as far as I was concerned, I had none. The ground beneath me that had always been sound and sure was gone. Stuck between those two extremes, I climbed into bed, pulled up the covers, shut the drapes, and disappeared from the world.

Why not? What was there to engage in? I was single and uninterested in starting a new social life. I did not have a show. And I had folded my company, freeing myself from the responsibility of salaries, office space, and development work, all of which went nowhere. I was completely unplugged from everything and everyone except one person—myself.

Days went by. Several months passed. I lived what I call my Dark Ages. I could not understand why nothing had grown from the many seeds I had planted in seemingly fertile ground. I had nothing else to give, and every day I reminded myself of that by going through the roll call of my life.

Marriage: Nope.

Work: Nope.

Spirit: Nope . . . Didn't have anything left to give.

Church: Nope.

Reading my Word: Nope.

Praying: Nope . . . I did not see the point. Was anyone listening?

I thought there was merit to being real with God and literally saying out loud to him, as I routinely did, "You know my heart. You know all of this. None of this is taking You by surprise.

121

But it's taking me by surprise. And I'm horribly disappointed by where Your plan has taken me."

I never said the word *depressed*. I never claimed depression as the reason I had hung a Closed sign on my door. But I was horribly disappointed. Horribly disappointed. I could not understand how I had gotten to this place or how He had allowed for this to happen. I know this happens to people. You run out of explanations. You cannot find the pieces to the puzzle. You look up and wonder. You ask questions. You begin to doubt. I would sit in my bed and run through my resume with Him: "I'm a tither. I go to church on Sunday. I serve at church. I'm public about your goodness. I never take credit for anything I do. I give You the glory. I'm one of your daughters. And this is how I'm treated? I don't understand."

My mom was one of the few people I allowed to see me like this. "I'm just being real," I told her one day. "I'm being real with myself—and God. I'm not trying to put on any front right now. It's enough for me to just inhale and exhale." She held my hand, fixed me lunch, and made sure she hugged me before she left. I appreciated the way she respected where I was. She didn't tell me what to do. She did not try to make me feel better, convince me I was mistaken, talk me to death because she was nervous or uncomfortable herself or load me up with Scriptures—or all the phrases that are not necessarily Scripture but that church folk know to say. She would just be with me.

A couple of friends also filled that role. They came, visited, made me feel loved and not abandoned. Not one person gave me a pity party. When you're going through something like this, you do not need friends that criticize or want to marry their misery to yours. Mine were there to listen and talk. My friend Andrea Mellini spoke metaphorically about stagnant water, reminding me that a puddle can be a temporary nuisance or a breeding ground for diseases. "You got a minute to be like this, sis," she said. "Just be mindful. Don't live in this space."

* * *

My exit from this woeful way station was abrupt and unantici-pated, catching even me by surprise when it happened. It was daytime, though you would not have known it with the drapes pulled in my bedroom, and I was watching a talk show on TV. Liza Minnelli was being interviewed. I think she was promot-ing a return to the stage, but what I remember more clearly is the way she spoke about battling various personal demons as a precursor to this latest comeback of hers. She was raw, fragile, strong, and inspiring all at the same time.

I sat up in bed and listened intently as she described her breakthrough. She said that she had revisited the work of her father, Vincente Minnelli, the great movie director whose films included *An American in Paris*, *Gigi*, *Father of the Bride*, and *Meet Me in St. Louis*. That surprised me, as I expected her to have said something about her mother, Judy Garland. But she didn't. She spoke about her father's work and wrapped up by saying, "I realized I come from that stock."

That hit me as really powerful and something clicked. I had a revelation, and it immediately recharged my battery. I got out of bed, opened the drapes, and walked outside into my back-yard. From there, I had a view of nearby oak and eucalyptus trees and beyond them, the Verdugo Mountains, which were shades of green, brown, purple. The sky was blue streaked with long strands of white clouds. As I took all this in, I heard Liza's voice in my head. "This is my father's work. I come from this stock."

Who would have thought Liza Minnelli would be the one to get me out of my Dark Ages? I was and am forever grateful for her transparency.

For the next few weeks, I took baby steps. Just one foot in front of the other. I did not try to walk a mile so to speak. One step was fine with me. It was a start. One step begets another step. I opened my drapes. I called friends. I went on walks to look at the trees and the mountains, listen to the birds, and bathe in the sunshine. "I know this is You," I said to God. "I know this is where I come from."

I had started locking my hair under Regine's wigs during the last season of *Living Single*. I wanted Kim to have her own identity and look apart from Regine. I had even started lightening my hair slowly . . . baby steps. I adored the look of locks, and wanted to include the natural hair path as a part of my journey. I also wanted to make sure I had a different look and vibe from the other actresses and celebs out there. Coming out of my Dark Ages, I regarded my new crown with a new energy of caring for myself, for my hair, for my spirit. Letting the hot waters flow through my hair was soothing and the cleansing element transcended a shower and gave me new life to wash away what wasn't working for me. I began to really get the concept that your hair is an extension (no pun intended) of you—your soul—if you allow it to be.

At the same time, my thirst for the Word returned. I opened my Bible and read a few sentences at a time. Random readings turned into pointed searches. I thought about David, my biblical hero, and sought out the passages in Psalms where he confronts his troubled soul, asking in Psalm 42:5: "Why are you so discontent? What's wrong with you, soul?" He says, "Oh my soul, why are you this way?" I asked the same of my soul. I examined my own past, as one does when finding themselves in unexpected places, and wondered where I had made mistakes. I began to question the hope and trust I had placed in God and started running down my resume, as I had so often in the past, when suddenly I caught myself. I stopped and instead ran down God's resume, specifically His track record with me, and then I shut up.

Years later, when my husband, the marvelous and all-wise Christopher Morgan, saw me slipping back into one of those periods of disappointment, he put his hand up like traffic cop and stopped me in my place. "Baby," he said, "you can't worry and remember at the same time." Meaning that I was either going to worry about things that have not yet happened or I could remember all the blessings, the stock, and what He has done. But I could not do both.

David's struggle helped guide me through my own journey of doubt. Weary and weak from groaning, his pillow drenched with tears, he still praised God, knowing that was the only way to get to the other side of his anguish. Again in Psalm 43:5, he puts his soul in check: "Why, my soul, are you downcast? Why so disturbed within me? Put your hope in God, for I will yet praise him, my Savior and my God." I got it; I knew the actions I had to take. Though frustrated, confused, and disappointed, I was not going to abandon my faith. Nor was I going to lie in bed and criticize and complain to God. I had been doing that, which left me one option, the only one that made sense. I praised Him. I read. I prayed. And I praised Him.

And as I did, gradually, I felt the woe-is-me worries that had been weighing me down begin to disappear. This is the beauty and power of saying, "I will yet praise Him." I quit focusing on excuses and looking for blame. I stopped punishing myself. I stopped counting what I did not have and instead counted the blessings that were mine. Yet, I praised Him.

And my load began to lighten.

My perspective began to change.

The lights came on.

I started looking out the window again.

By the spring, I had reconnected with my agents and started reading scripts and going on auditions. No one was happier to hear this than my mom. "Are you back?" she asked one day as we caught up on the phone. "I don't know," I said. "But I'm dressed, smelling good, and ready for when the time comes."

* * *

In May, the time came. It was my thirtieth birthday. As far as the world was concerned, I still did not look more than twenty, but inside I was excited about the step up into this new decade. I was one of those people—not necessarily one of those women, just one of those people in general—who felt thirty was *the* decade to be my best. It was about adulthood, independence, freedom, and hopefully confidence. To prepare, I did something bold, drastic, and wonderful. I dyed my locks nearly platinum blond. No more baby steps.

Look, if you're not in therapy, the beauty salon can be the perfect place to find your footing after a breakup or a breakdown. Or it can be a disaster. At first, my stylist reacted like it was the latter. To her, I was conservative Kimmy. But my explanation changed her opinion. "No, I made the decision," I said. "I'm turning thirty. It's time to come out of hiding. It's time to do something different." The transformation was immediate, and I loved it. I felt lighter. My spirit felt lighter. Like I could breathe and just be, in a word, easier. At the same time I felt very empowered, incredibly strong. Dare I say glimpses of a boldness were starting to enter my radar?

If that was me coming out of my shell, I also stepped forward as a political activist, a slightly different space from being a part of political campaigns. Three days before my birthday, I was among forty-six people arrested outside a Riverside courthouse, protesting a judge's decision to not charge four police officers for killing nineteen-year-old Tyisha Miller after finding her unconscious in her car. The incident had happened in December. Miller had been driving her aunt's car late at night with a teenage friend, and they got a flat tire. After her friend returned from getting help, Miller was unconscious in the driver's seat with the engine running and the radio on. According to reports, she was comatose, with foam oozing from her mouth. A gun was also on the seat next to her.

Police were summoned—and four arrived within minutes. Because of the gun on her seat, they approached the car with their own guns drawn. Unable to rouse her, and seeing she needed emergency medical help, they broke the window. At that point, Miller supposedly awakened, reached for her gun, and the officers shot her twenty-three times. The community was outraged by the incident and further incensed when an investigation called the action an error in judgment rather than a crime, or more specifically, a homicide.

A local judge concurred, and that is when I responded to the call to join a protest outside the courthouse. Hundreds of others turned out and we stood in front of the police station chanting, "No justice! No peace!" Many of us were arrested, including Reverend Al Sharpton, comedian-activist Dick Gregory, Martin Luther King III, Sandra Moore from CORE, and myself. It was intense. The rage from both protestors and police was like a keg of dynamite on the verge of exploding.

It was scary, like nothing I'd ever been a part of. This was seven years after Rodney King had been beaten by police and touched off riots across Los Angeles. Just three months earlier, an unarmed twenty-three-year-old black man named Amadou Diallo was shot forty-one times by officers outside his apartment in New York while reaching for his wallet. I knew the possibility existed that something similar could happen to me, my teenage sister, or one of my friends simply for the color of our skin, and if it did, there was a high probability that those involved would not be held responsible. Why? Because they were white.

And that is why I stood outside the Riverside police headquarters when the call went out for protestors. The lesson I'd learned from Jesse Jackson and those of his generation who had marched in Birmingham, Selma, and Washington was that change only happens if you show up.

Days later, I celebrated my actual birthday in St. Lucia, a paradise of gorgeous sandy beaches and lush, green mountains in the Caribbean. After receiving an invitation from BET and the St. Lucia tourist board to be their guest at the island's annual jazz festival, I went there with a sisterfriend to keep me company. Luckily, she was an independent and understanding type because I met a handsome young man whose family owned a resort there and indulged in a fun-in-the-sun romance to go with my new blond locks. We went horseback riding on the beach, explored hidden canyons, swam in calm pools under dramatic waterfalls, enjoyed romantic candlelit dinners, and saw live shows with David Sanborn, Patti LaBelle, and my friend Malcolm-Jamal Warner, who tore it up with his band.

I had such a good time that I continued going to St. Lucia for my birthday for the next few years. My mom was delighted when I told her about my island boyfriend. "Well, you know, honey, Jesus's people didn't take Him in," she said. "He had to go far away to get Him some love, too."

16

Scrappy

It was a beautiful day, one of those afternoons that make living in California feel like paradise, and I returned home from a hike in a nearby canyon, hot and sweaty. I drank half a glass of ice water, put it down on the kitchen counter, patted some sweat off my face, and looked at myself in the mirror. I was not the athletic type on a regular basis, but a little exercise felt good, and it looked good. I had on a pink T-shirt and sweatpants. My hair was a little messy, but my blonde locks gave me a sort of sexy Shari Belafonte glow, emphasis on *sort of*. "But I'll take it," I said.

I was enjoying the way thirty and then thirty-one felt, even if I was painfully aware that my exit from the Dark Ages was made by taking baby steps. For one thing, there was the lack of a relationship. I was ready and open to meeting someone special, and I was looking, but my prince was nowhere in sight. Then there was work, which consisted of a little bit of everything. I directed an episode of the Nickelodeon series *100 Deeds for Ed-*

die McDowd. I guested on the Lifetime series *Strong Medicine* and took a part in a cute, small-budget coming-of-age movie called *Glow*.

I probably did my best dramatic work on a TV movie titled *Hidden Blessings*. Starring Cynda Williams and Marc Gomes, it was a suspenseful BET movie about a female cop who falls in love with an architect accused of killing his wife. I played his assistant, who, it turned out, actually committed the murder. I had worked with the director, Timothy Wayne Folsome, on *Uninvited Guest*, and he allowed me the room to discover and shape my character. I am sure he picked up on how much I enjoyed being in a drama. It was a different playground for me.

But it was only a couple of weeks of shooting, and then I was back home, waiting for the next opportunity. Whether in front of the camera or behind it, jobs were few and far between. This was a difficult reality for me to deal with. It was not like I woke from a dark period, left my bedroom, and everything magically changed. My agents were not sitting on offers. No one was writing a series for me. My accountant was not on the phone telling me I had no worries.

No, instead I stepped back into real life. One step at a time. Like every other actor in Hollywood, I had to hustle and hope, and when I got work, I praised God, called my mom, and jumped up and down the way I used to when I was a little kid and one of us booked a job. At one point, I did think about trying to get a job in development at NBC. It seemed stable. In reality, it was probably as fraught with insecurity as any other job in the creative field. But when I looked inside myself, I did not just see an actor. I saw the soul of an artist. Like it or not, I was a performer—and the truth was, I loved it. I said to myself, "Yes, this life can be excruciating. But this is my life. This is the life I chose. This is the life that feels right for me."

Everyone has these moments of questioning their path. God knows, I had mine. I asked the questions. I listened for a response. I heard my inner voice provide the answers. "You're an actress." I knew it was not easy—not now or ever. I wanted things to be sure. But life was not about certainty. I wanted to know why it felt like I was constantly having to prove myself. But who doesn't have to prove themselves every day in one way or another? Who doesn't have to dig in?

I was scrappy. I liked that about myself. I liked that word—*scrappy*. I had thought of myself in that way for years. But now, in my thirties, it really fit. As did so many other things. Everyone goes through periods when they ask, Am I good enough? Am I pretty enough? Am I sexy enough? Am I smart enough? Am I black enough? Am I funny enough? Are my boobs enough? Is my butt enough? Is my car enough? Is my bank account enough? Oh my God, I had asked those questions, too—and then some. The answers were not always what I wanted to hear. This time, though, I told myself, "You know what? You are enough the way you are. More than enough."

Translation: No matter how much I struggled between jobs, no matter how much I wished I had steady work, no matter how much I wanted to have a great man in my life, no matter how much I wished I was taller, smarter, richer, prettier, whatever, I liked who I was, and that kept me afloat and looking forward.

I hiked.

I read.

I recarpeted my bedroom floor.

I hung out with friends.

I saw my family.

I went to church.

I locked my hair—and hair is key, isn't it?

I was transforming inside and out. Reinvention was in the air and I was taking deep breaths, drinking in change. My hair was the giveaway.

I was connecting more and more with a bohemian vibe.

I was getting comfortable in my skin.

I was living my life—really making a conscious effort to live—as best I could.

* * *

Then the phone rang. It was work. I went to Chicago for a three-week run in *The Vagina Monologues*. It was summer 2001, and I arrived on one of those hot, sticky days I remembered all too well from when I used to visit Jonathan Jackson and his family. But I was ecstatic to be there. I loved Chicago. I also loved the play. *The Vagina Monologues* was a tremendous piece of work about femininity, self-esteem, sex, reproduction, the strength of women, what it meant to be a woman, independence, politics, and life. I was all in. The subject, the fit, and the timing all worked for me.

* * *

Theater in the summertime traditionally does not do well because everyone is outside having fun. Seats often go unfilled. So I appreciated that the show's producer, Rob Colson, tapped me in the hope of that not being the case, and it wasn't. We had a tremendous turnout. I also had some very good friends in Chicago who took me out to cool neighborhood hot spots whenever I had free time. One night they introduced me to spoken-word poetry. It was open mic night at a club. I was enthralled. Not every person was great, but many were, and I appreciated what it took for each person to get up there and present their words on that otherwise bare stage.

"Oh my gosh, this is fantastic," I kept saying to my friends, without mentioning the pull I immediately felt to get up there myself. It was as if the words were already poised at the tip of my tongue.

Forget baby steps. Forget glimpses of boldness. Getting up there would be a giant leap off a cliff. But I knew I had to do it. I knew I would do it. The play had given me a new level of confidence in terms of doing monologues onstage with only a microphone. Years earlier, while on the road in a play called *One Monkey Don't Stop No Show*, I had a small monologue in the middle of the show. Ron Milner, the great playwright, was the director, and he spent days working with me on that small but significant portion because I was horribly uncomfortable standing onstage by myself, talking to the audience.

I was used to working with other people, playing off them, and being able to stop and redo if I messed up. The vulnerability of flying solo unnerved me. For many actors, that is part of the thrill of doing theater. I enjoyed that rush, too; it just required a lot of internal pushing to get me to that point. Doing *The Vagina Monologues* liberated me from some of that fear. The words Eve Ensler had written were empowering, personally and professionally. I could feel the audience react and used their energy to get me past my fear. Then I wanted more.

As I digested that spoken-word experience, I could feel my inner poet emerging from my soul. It was being drawn out by a beautiful memory I had of seeing the incomparable Ruby Dee in her one-woman show, *My One Good Nerve: A Visit with Ruby Dee*. In it, she talked about her life, played numerous characters, and dished up commentary on all that mattered. "Love is when you sink into his arms, and end up with your arms in the sink," she said. How many years earlier had I seen her perform that piece? Maybe five. Maybe four. Yet her poet prowess was indelible and intoxicating, and it was calling mine forth.

A few days later, I went back to the club with my friends. I was ready to take my turn onstage. I'd journaled in a pretty little notebook for years, filling it with thoughts and feelings that I realized I had written in verse-like fragments. As I prepared for my debut, I reworked some of those lines into very personal pieces.

To mitigate my nervousness, I called myself Blondielocks. Even with that pen name, I was still Kim, and I was still shaking from the inside out. What I said was not anything a writer gave me. Those lines were my thoughts, my creativity, my soul, and oh my God, I might as well have walked onstage butt naked. I could not have felt more exposed. In the intro to one of her songs, my dear sisterfriend Erykah Badu said, "I'm an artist, and I'm sensitive about my *##%." It was one of the greatest, truest lines I had ever heard, and it described the way I felt as I recited a piece called "Exotic or Toxic."

Exotic or toxic
Which will you be?
To my mind,
My body, my soul,
To me?

Exotic or toxic?

Exotic like a faraway land,
Like Never-Never Land . . .
Or toxic like a man who is still a boy,
Like Peter Pan?

It was an exploration of all those questions you ask when you meet a man who jump-starts your heart. My recitation was a performance. It may have seemed like I was doing a character, but it was actually me; a part of me came out when I spit my words. Intense, passionate, dramatic, angry, soft, I took the audience—and myself—for a ride, especially with this one, which reopened some old wounds. After several minutes, I came to an abrupt stop. "*Exotic or toxic?*"

I lowered my head and stared at the rug covering the hard boards of the stage. I closed my eyes. I took a deep breath, which felt like the first one I had taken in a week. Then, from within the faraway place I had gone to recover, I heard a noise—applause. Ah, sweet applause, the lifeblood of a performer. The response was fantastic. I looked up, smiling, and had my Sally Field moment where, feeling relief and satisfaction, I thought, *They like it. They really like it.*

And they liked me. Imagine that. Drink that in, sister. This was not Tootie they were clapping for. Nor was it Regine. I didn't recite lines from their writers. It was me, Kim, performing *my* words . . . channeling my poet world, and wow, they liked me. They really liked me.

After that I dove in headfirst. I wrote nonstop and read as often as I could. I had to buy another journal and soon, another one. Emboldened, I had a longtime guy friend in Chicago whom I looked at one night when we were out having dinner and wondered aloud, "What do you think a romantic version of us would look like?" I do not think I would have had the nerve to go there if not for the poetry. We tried it. He gave me a beautiful crystal vase, which I filled with flowers.

A week later, we started to realize that romantic territory was not a good fit for us, and lo and behold, the vase he gave me broke. Instead of cleaning up the mess, I ran for my journal. That night I stepped onstage at a club out in the suburbs. It was another open mic night. He was in the audience and heard me read this brand-new piece I had titled, "The Vase You Gave Me Broke Last Night, Is It a Sign?"

> Heart and soul were just talking about you the other day, wondering if there would be a sign, and then the vase you gave me broke.

As I sat back down at our table, he shook his head in what appeared to be admiration. It could also have been amusement. A waitress brought me a glass of water and complimented my piece. After she left, my friend gave my hand an affectionate squeeze. "You're so deep," he said, smiling. "And, no, it wasn't a sign."

* * *

Following the play, I kept busy with cameos on various sitcoms. I also spent three glorious weeks in San Francisco for *Me & Mrs. Jones*, an indie feature that was a vitamin shake for my ego. Described by *Variety* as "a mix of romantic comedy and boss-from-hell shenanigans," and costarring Brian White and Wanda Christine, it was about a hot young graphic artist (Brian) at an online dating service whose boss (Wanda) takes an interest in him, and vice versa, until Mr. Hot Stuff comes upon my flashy self. The director Ed Laborde specifically asked for me. I was ecstatic to be tapped for a part that framed my thirty-two-year-old behind as desirable—er, irresistible.

I ate it up. I was a leading lady. I was also in a movie that was not a stereotypical "black" story. Movies like *Love & Basketball*, *Waiting to Exhale*, *Eve's Bayou*, anything from Spike Lee, and *Me & Mrs. Jones* showed there were many meaningful, profound, romantic, dramatic, and lovely human stories to tell featuring African Americans. There just weren't enough of them—not in theaters or on TV.

The issue was a personal one. I had spent fifteen years on TV and I benefited from name recognition. I never felt anything less than loved, but rarely did I feel *wanted* by the industry where I had spent half my life. Why else was I not working more often? How else could I explain that I was not auditioning for comedies about black families or being called in to play a doctor on a new hospital drama? The fact was, Hollywood just didn't have enough jobs for black people. Not for me—and not for any of the other actors, writers, producers, and directors of color.

That was one of the motivations behind the production company I'd started. I wanted to create roles for actors like me. I wanted to tell stories that were going untold. Only in retrospect did I see the obstacles were greater than I imagined and more powerful than little ol' me could overcome. But that did not mean I gave up. I was still here—still looking, fighting, and kicking. Still scrappy. I told myself there was a cycle. You finish a series, then you have a small drought, then there is a whole bunch of guest-starring work, and then another series comes along. I imagined that I was in the guest-starring phase before that next big thing came along.

The system, like society itself, was weighted to squeeze the self-worth we had as African Americans. I refused to accept it. Maybe it was because I was older, more confident, and more determined, but instead of retreating to my bedroom as I had before, I continued to create. Work was my way of fighting back. I directed the Nickelodeon series *Taina* and an issue-oriented syndicated daytime series called *Teen Talk*. I worked on an indie film in New York until financing fell through at the tenth hour. I did another play in Detroit.

But the most satisfying work I did at the time continued to be my spoken word, which I took to smooth jazz festivals. I did festivals in Mexico and the Bahamas. I went back to St. Lucia. I opened for trumpeter Rick Braun. Working the stage in front of my band, my thing was part performance, part therapy, and part primal rant. *I'm still here. I ain't going anywhere. I'm still creating. You will not lock me out or shut me up. I am better than ever. In fact, when you look at me, you'll see what I see: there's more of me to be. More of me to be.*

Perhaps this line of thinking was my version of a sentiment to come forth years later in the hit musical *Hamilton*, with the song "The Room Where It Happens." I sat riveted throughout the show, and when I heard that song, all I could think was, *If I'm not in the room where it happens, I'll make my own room where it happens.*

* * *

Indeed. In 2003, I collaborated with singer-trumpeter Johnny Britt and rapper-singer Sean E. Mac, better known as the smooth jazz–hip hop duo Impromp2, on a cut about a fictional spoken-word poet who went by the name of Mocha Soul. "Mocha Soul, that's me," I purred. "Speakin' my truth into the wind, I'm finally comfortable in my skin . . . " I was supposed to be creating a character, but I couldn't hold back the autobiography. I poured a lot of myself into it, and as I did, unavoidably, I began to think about cutting my own album.

It seemed like a daunting project until inspiration hit. I was in IKEA of all places, looking for a side table. As I walked from the area with living room furniture into the section with accent pieces, I had a vision—an ecstatic vision like none other in my experience. I saw the album almost in its entirety, complete and whole, right in front of me. It was just there, as in front of me as the storage unit I grabbed hold of to steady myself. I grabbed one of those little yellow pencils and a handful of small notepads they provide to write on and I practically wrote the entire album that eventually became *Smooth Is Spoken Here.*

Crazy, right?

Soon I was in the studio with musician friends. I did not write music, but I was able to communicate the sounds I heard in my head to the great players I worked with, and they turned those rhythmic musings into eleven tracks, including "Playtime," "Swanky," "HarlemHoney," "The Cool-Out Spot," and "Smooth Is Spoken Here." My dear friend, superstar saxohonist Najee and poet C.O.C.O. Brown were among those who generously added their gifts. And yes, the album had a definite vibe, which one New York paper called "a dynamic collaboration of music and poetry." Thank you.

A limited run of CDs were made and sold through Carol's Daughter, the online retail store founded by our family friend

Lisa Price, and on my own website. When the CDs were gone, they were gone—that was it. For me, it was enough to have made the album. But I continued to tour and share my spoken-word poetry. In 2005, I went on HBO's *Russell Simmons Def Poetry Jam*. I had been a fan of the show since its debut in 2002 and applauded HBO for putting it on the air. Though purists criticized the show, I was in from the debut episode. It put amazing poets and spoken word artists in front of a broad audience and gave us a podium on which we could stand and speak freely of every aspect of our lives. Where else could you hear Nikki Giovanni, Georgia Me, and Sonia Sanchez? These were our voices, and not watered down by a network's commercial sensibilities and needs. I mean the fourth episode featured Dave Chappelle and Amiri Baraka reading his powerful piece "Why Is We Americans?"

This was powerful stuff. Just WOW stuff.

He was speaking to us—and for us.

And it was on TV!

By the time I went on the show, I was aware of the high bar that had been set. I worked out my piece at the Conga Room in LA. It was titled "How Come? (War Cry of the Single Woman)" and it was a big, sprawling, angry, reflective work meant to challenge myself as much as it did those on the receiving end. I flew to New York and went onstage draped in a beautiful, floor-length green and gold dress, with my blond locks and swag fully on. I glared at the audience just long enough for them to get the message that they weren't about to hear Tootie or Regine. Then I started:

HOW COME? (War Cry of the Single Woman)
Well maybe it's not you, it's them
Maybe they're scared
Maybe they're intimidated
Maybe they're gun-shy

Maybe I'm tired of them crutches,
Weak excuses, but too scared to grab a gun and fire!

HOW COME
I can cook my butt off,
talk cars,
sports,
politics
wax it with passion,
yo,
and still single?
Will cook catfish naked in high heels
and love like a champ,
give them fever...

HOW COME
"Oh well baby, you too good for me.
Uh baby, I don't deserve you."
Don't settle for that come up.
Step up.

HOW COME
You respond with,
"You trying to change me?"

HOW COME
You weren't ready and wanted to "just be friends"
when I perfectly rolled a tree on the first try
because I heard you say that's the sexiest thing a sister
could do for her man?

HOW COME
You don't realize and don't remember that the King
Is supposed to be with the Queen,

Scrappy

Not the court jester?

HOW COME
I heard that after 9/11 folks got more committed to life,
love, spirit, family?
Are we saying that tragedy and fear should jump-start
    the heart?
We mustn't forget these classic crutches
and excuses:
"Uh, I had a messed up childhood" (who hasn't?)
"Uh, well I've been hurt real bad" (who hasn't?)
"Oh, well, baby, you know what, baby, you see the time
    is not right,
see the time is not right,
see I wanna be in a certain place
financially,
emotionally,
spiritually."
"Yeah, well, baby, most people are divorced,
and if they are together they ain't happy."
So?
And?

Have we forgotten y'all that once upon a time
high school sweethearts who met in third grade
got married and they built a life
and shared a life
and set and met goals
and loved with souls

Is that a fairy tale lived long ago?
I don't know.
How far away from that do we go to get back to that?
Because you know

History does repeat itself

HOW COME
we can't meet each other in the middle
with our fears and our hang-ups and our issues?

HOW COME
We can't meet each other in the middle
And live and love
And live and love
And live and love?

HOW COME?

That Still, Small Voice

17

Get in the Passenger Seat and Let God Drive

I remember when "How Come" first came out of me. It was a few months before I performed it on *Def Poetry Jam*. I sat on my bedroom floor, exhausted from shouting and crying those words into my little recorder. I had recently ended a two-year relationship for which I'd had oh-so-high hopes. The two of us were not able to get on the same page in terms of having life goals and a family together. It had been a painful last conversation for both of us; my spirit was so heavy and my heart was still wounded. With my face buried in my hands, I asked, "How come it didn't work out?"

I was speaking specifically—and generally.

I was speaking for myself. I was speaking for so many others.

It was light outside, the late afternoon. I walked outside and looked around the backyard. My gaze fell upon a neighbor's jacaranda tree. Its branches rose above the fence. Full of leaves and purple flowers, it looked like the kind of impressionist tree Monet would have created had he lived in LA. It was beautiful. I did not want to carry around the heaviness of a wounded heart. I remember being on the phone with a girlfriend and saying, "I'm over it. Done with it."

Such outbursts were uncharacteristic, but I needed to vent. "He wasn't the one," I continued. "Neither was the other guy. I don't get it. I'm not a crazy chick. I'm not one of those women about whom people say, 'Oh, watch out for her.' Maybe I'm just part of a generation that has some bad women who screwed it up for those of us who are good. That's it. There are bad women out there messing it up for us good ones."

My friend laughed. "You sound like you're spittin' on *Def Poetry* again," she said.

I summoned a half-smile. "I'm definitely spittin'," I said.

Ready to start building something and willing to shake things up, I put my house up for sale and began traveling to Tampa, Florida, intending to purchase five or ten acres. Land was cheap there, cheaper than in LA. I wanted to build a house—or an ark. Or something. I had no intention of giving up acting, directing, or producing, but my agenda now included other goals.

Like opening a juice bar. Why not? I figured I would write my next TV series there, too. And if I met a man, well, I had mixed feelings about another relationship, obviously, and would deal with the situation when and if it happened.

But one thing stood above all else. It was more of a question than an actual objective, and the question was this: What about kids? I had asked that question before, when I was in a relationship, and it seemed more feasible. Now, in my midthirties, I wanted certain parts of my life fulfilled, and having children was on my list. It was, in fact, high up on my list. I never subscribed to the ticking biological clock. I trusted that God knew my heart. I wanted my Partner in Life & Love...I wanted Husband. I wanted to be Wife. I wasn't rocking rose-colored glasses. I didn't simply want the roles or labels. I also wanted the work that came with them.

One day I was having lunch with my friend, music producer Carvin Haggins, and though I was seated across a small table, he could see my mind was elsewhere. Apparently I had muttered something as he was talking to me. "I was thinking about children," I said. "Let's say I don't meet anyone and I want to have a baby—or babies—on my own. How do I even go about it? Do I make a short list of my male friends whom I love and adore and tell 'em, 'Hey, no strings attached'? Or do I adopt?"

Carvin sat back and rubbed his chin in thought. We talked about dating and relationships, before moving the conversation onto other topics. He had several projects. I'd been on several auditions. "My foot is on the gas," I said, "but the car is still in neutral." He sympathized. Show business is a collaborative business, requiring many people at different levels to buy into a project before it gets off the ground, which is sort of like everything in life.

I sighed. Carvin reminded me that Jesus was thwarted time and again. I nodded and repeated something that Pastor Joel Osteen had once said: "Hang on to your faith. It may not look like there's a way, but God still has a way." And that is essentially what Carvin told me. He said, "Kim, my friend, get back in the passenger seat and let God drive the car."

I got it.

Take a deep breath.

Loosen your grip.

Let life happen.

Then be ready when it does happen.

* * *

And so I was.

It was April 2005, and I had sold my house, put my belongings in storage, and moved in with my mom and dad. I did not like the idea of moving in with my parents at age thirty-six, but my monthly jaunts to Florida and side trips to New York, Chicago, and Detroit for work and appearances or meetings ensured I was more of a visitor than a semipermanent squatter. On the plus side, they were a supportive cheering section. When I booked a pilot for a sitcom based on the rapper Bow Wow and his mother, my mom and I jumped up and down, hugged, and hollered the way we did in 1976 after I booked my Mrs. Butterworth's commercial (and every time since). It was the way we were and would always be.

Of course, my mom, being the way *she* is, took the celebration a touch too far. My bathroom at her house had an enormous mirror over the double sinks, and she wrote in red, *Dressed-to-Kill*-style lipstick across the entire thing: "Welcome back to television." It scared the crap out of me when I walked in and turned on the light. Who does that? I could not even read it at first; I thought I had a stalker.

Days later, I flew to Atlanta to hang out with Bow's mom and research the role. The sitcom pilot focused more on her than her famous son as she transitioned from being a mom and manager to just a manager. With more time on her hands, she opened an upscale boutique and began to date. Upon meeting, the two of us bonded immediately over being single and the dating scene. "I'm frustrated and honestly, I'm over it," I told her. "Amen," she said.

"I'm done with the litany of excuses and justifications," I continued, "the reasoning and quote-unquote logic of why things just aren't right."

"Amen," she said again.

Who was researching whom, right?

Anyway, a friend of mine who was in the play *Five Guys Named Moe* had invited me to dinner with some of his cast mates. I said sure. We were all in the same hotel across from the Alliance Theater where the show was being done. We met in my friend's suite. It was Friday night, and as I stepped in the room and walked toward them, I saw my friend talking to one of his cast mates, or rather my eyes landed on the guy my friend was talking to, because I have no recollection of seeing my friend or anyone else at that instant, only this new, very handsome man. I felt my heart flutter and actually said to myself, "My God, who is that?"

Looking back, it is an example of God's bigger plan. It has to be. I had nothing in mind other than dinner at Houlihan's and maybe, if I am completely open, nibbling some firecracker chicken if someone else ordered it, but otherwise sticking to a low-fat, healthy diet. Instead I got a teeming, three-course serving of the witty, charismatic, sexy man who would become my husband and the father of my children.

His name was Christopher L. Morgan. He walked me down the street to the restaurant, standing on the outside like a gentleman. I noticed. He was old school. At the restaurant, he stepped forward and held the door open for me. Again, I noticed; the man was also courteous and gallant. Chivalry was not dead. At the table, he sat across from me and I swear, the man had swag even while sitting down.

He also had army-green-brown eyes that were impossibly mesmerizing. I had never seen anything like them. We talked throughout dinner. He was witty and funny as all get-out. His references were also spot-on, brilliant, and old school. He seemed to have an old soul, which resonated with me, as did so much about him that night, including that he had recently worked with my beloved friend, Blair, in an Off-Broadway production of Ossie Davis's play *Purlie*.

Before the evening was over, they invited me to their rehearsal the following morning. Though I was leaving that Saturday afternoon, I accepted the offer, and I am forever grateful I did. I got to see Christopher L. Morgan perform. It was magic. It was breathtaking. As a performer, I've always been all about the craft, and I could see that was also at Chris's core. He was in full possession of his craft, to the point where he turned it into pure artistry. He was in the moment, and he rendered me literally breathless.

I was able to steal myself away long enough to call Blair in Los Angeles. Despite the three-hour time difference, which made it ridiculously early out there, he answered. That is when you know somebody really loves you. I said, "Hey, bro, do you remember meeting this brother when you guys worked together a month or two ago on *Purlie*?"

Blair said, "Yeah. Chris Morgan. Hell of a dancer. Good brother. And he's from Virginia so you know he's cool."

"Okay, thanks," I said.

Suddenly Blair sounded more awake. "Why do you want to know?" he asked.

"I just met him," I said. "And I'm just wondering."

"Uh, all right," he said. "Good guy. Tell him hello."

I did more than that. After getting Blair's quasi-seal of approval, I slipped my number into Chris's backpack, carefully putting it next to his wallet to ensure that he would see it. Then I left for the airport, expecting to hear from him in a day or two. When the phone did not ring after the third day, I began to wonder what was going on. Thankfully, God was merciful and kept me busy with work on the Bow pilot. Still, when I did not hear from Chris after a week, I called our mutual friend in Atlanta and asked if he knew whether Chris had received my note.

"Yeah, he got it," my friend said—and it killed him to hear the disappointed tone in my voice when I said, "Oh." He could hear my heart sinking like an anchor dropped into the ocean without a rope attached. For my own well-being, I decided at that point to leave it alone and go about my business. And it was not like I was thinking anything long-term yet. Heck no. I wanted more of that feeling I had sitting next to him in the restaurant, more of that feeling of fun, excitement, curiosity, and what I thought was a mutual attraction. Whatever.

On day ten, though, the phone rang. "Hey, it's me—Chris." He sounded all full of innocence and charm. My feeling was— and still is—hey, acknowledge that you at least received the information. I thought I was clever sliding my number into his bag and next to his wallet to make sure he would get it. But then to just have radio silence? *You ain't got nothing to say? Not even nice to meet you?* Chris's side is that he did not want to come off as too eager. He thought he was playing it cool by waiting. "Hey, it's me—Kim," I said icily, and then, with that out of the way, we talked for two hours.

* * *

Chris's play officially opened in early May, which happened to fall on my birthday, and I returned to Atlanta to spend that special time with him. We planned it as a grown-up weekend— a weekend of fun and then deuces. I knew it wasn't in line with my belief system, but this was the reality of my life as an adult woman in her middle thirties. After a touchy breakup and a failed marriage, I did not believe I was going to have that special someone in my life, and Chris, who had just gotten divorced after ten years of marriage, felt similarly.

Therein was the problem. When it was time to say goodbye at the end of the weekend, neither one of us wanted to let go. This was not the sentiment you were supposed to have after a— and pardon me for saying it like this—after a hit-it-and-quit-it weekend. And it was not that we simply wanted to hit it again. No, we realized that we liked each other as people, as potential best friends for life. We sensed a match and the opportunity to build something together.

The next time I visited Atlanta, Chris's parents and his sister and brother-in-law had come to see him in the show. They had their newborn daughter with them. I happily volunteered to babysit so they could see how amazing Chris was in the show.

It also gave his family and me a chance to meet. I welcomed their scrutiny. I could see them giving me a long, careful look as a babysitter, and then the different but equally long and careful look as Chris's new love interest. They were great. I loved them. They were super protective of Chris, who was still healing from his breakup, but at the same time they got a sense of me as well as a sense of what Chris and I were developing. They saw happiness returning to his heart.

In the meantime, I shuttled between LA and New York, working on a handful of projects, including a documentary for BET Jazz on some rare recordings jazz giants Thelonious Monk and John Coltrane had made at Carnegie Hall. The recordings had turned up in the Library of Congress. My film chronicled the footage from discovery to restoration to a reissue of the music by Blue Note Records. I was not a jazz head, which was the reason BET had brought me on board. "You'll look at it through the lens of the masses," the executive told me.

Aside from being an extraordinary project, *Discovering Monk and Trane: One Night at Carnegie Hall* inadvertently helped focus my life. Till then, I was living at home, bopping off here and there for freelance directing gigs, and still traveling to Florida every month in search of property and my elusive juice store. The activity was great for my spirit. The busier my calendar, the better I felt. But as I worked on the *Monk and Trane* project and took meetings with the Caribbean Tourism Organization, I realized that I liked New York City. A lot.

"You should really think about moving back there," a close friend of mine said as I went on about the city's unique energy. "You're happy there. You love it. It could be really good for you. It could stir your pot, get some things moving in you again." He was right. I loved jumping on the subway, walking through Central Park, or heading uptown to a favorite little Caribbean restaurant in Harlem. But what about Florida? Indeed, what about Florida?

I had spent the past two years shopping for land there, except now when I shut my eyes and pictured myself behind the counter of a little juice bar and tending to a miniature ranch, it seemed absurd. *What am I going to do on five acres except leave all the lights on and sleep with my back against the front door?* I thought. *It's not like I have family or friends there.*

The difference was Christopher L. Morgan. After our grown-up weekend, we talked every day, often multiple times a day, and grew close quickly. In June, we got together in New York City. Chris had finished his gig in Atlanta and had only a few days in his schedule before he went to Kansas City for his next gig, a show called *From My Hometown*. He had to clear out his belongings from the apartment he had shared with his ex-wife. She had already moved her things.

I was in New York on business, staying downtown with a girlfriend—actually, the sister of my island romance from a few years earlier. Chris and I went out on a date. Beyond having a good time, we confirmed our mutual feeling of wanting to be together. Older and experienced, we both knew what we wanted—and needed—in a relationship. Over dinner and lunch the next day, and then walking uptown hand in hand on an early summer afternoon, Chris and I made it clear that what we wanted and needed in our lives was each other.

Later, after Chris had gone, I spent a few more days in New York. I thought about the way being with him made me feel. I also thought about the reality of making that work. Chris was booked most of the year, sometimes spending up to nine months on the road in plays. He based himself in New York. I loved the city, too. Unlike LA, where going anyplace meant getting into your car, dealing with traffic, and looking for a parking spot, I loved the freedom of being able to walk out my door and go to the store, a museum, a coffee shop, or wherever. I loved the change of seasons. I loved connecting to my roots. I loved sharing that with Chris.

After we agreed to never go more than two weeks without seeing each other, I visited Chris in Kansas City. He was still in rehearsals. If I was in a hotel for more than twenty-four hours, my way of settling in was to rearrange the furniture, something I did as Chris watched with some astonishment. When I finished, he was impressed. "What else you got up your sleeve?" he asked.

Nothing that I was ready to show him. In past relationships, I had been too eager to show that I would be a good wife and homemaker. I came on too strong. If I liked someone, I wanted them to see how I operated. It was too much and scared them right out of the relationship. I was a gale-force wind when a soft, warm breeze would have been more effective—and more seductive. With Chris, I played it cooler. I finally got the memo; it just arrived later in life.

But I knew what I wanted from this relationship. I wanted permanency. Chris was a keeper. My family had provided their seal of approval. My mom and Chris also had Virginia roots in common and shared a passion for musical theater. He had gone to James Madison University. He was a self-starter who kept a gig. He would be in a play for three months at a time and often have two or three lined up. Like me, he knew how to get his hustle on, and seemed to enjoy it.

One day later that summer I was back in Kansas City and hanging out in his hotel room. Chris had just come back from rehearsal and had plopped himself across the bed. I stared at him for a while in silence. My eyes roamed across his muscled body, from head to toe. Though we had known each other only four months, I felt like it had been a lifetime. Yet I knew that was wishful thinking. The time had passed in the blink of an eye. What I was feeling was the excitement of a lifetime ahead of us. I wanted to be together. Without the hassle of travel. And without the frustration of arranging long-distance phone calls. I took a deep breath. "Chris? You sleeping?" I said.

"No," he replied, turning his head slightly and looking at me through one eye. "What's up?"

"I'd like to share the same zip code with you," I said. "How do we do that and make it work so that you're comfortable with it, too?"

I about passed out as those words came out of my mouth. I thought the Lord was going to slap those sentences out of my mouth before I could say them. I had never lived with a man outside of my first husband. But I had never done a lot of things I did with Chris. I had never felt the way I felt when I was with him.

And now that I had put my cards on the table—let's say I showed him a full house—the next move was his.

18

Wife

Yeah, I'm with you," Chris said after sitting up in bed and thinking about it for a moment. "I get it. I see it. Let's do it."

From then on, the hunt was on. Once I began looking at apartments, though, I went straight to my sweet spot—Harlem. When I lived there from birth to age six, it was simply home, the place where I lived, and I never lost that sense of having lived there and calling it home. Over the years, I frequented the homes of friends who had moved there, restaurants that had opened, and shops and clubs. By 2005, Harlem was in the midst of yet another revitalization—not a renaissance per se, but a rediscovery. Space was limited in Manhattan. People with money were buying buildings and restoring the brownstones. Hip restaurants opened. Hearing about the places where I was looking at apartments, my mom marveled, "Your Harlem is not my Harlem."

To be sure, my Harlem was rebuilt and more racially diverse.

The streets were also safer than in the 1960s and '70s. Chris and I saw one place that was directly across the street from St. Nicholas Park, a walk-up whose listing made it sound full of potential. But when we got there, we saw it was next to an empty lot that was home to dozens of clucking chickens. Inside, the building had a pronounced tilt to it. "Is this place sinking?" Chris asked as we climbed the stairs.

"Or is it going to just fall down one day?" I asked.

The radiator in the bedroom had a janky sort of chain attaching it to a pole. I jangled it curiously; New York wasn't prone to earthquakes. "What's this?" I asked. "Handcuffs?"

Hearing that, Chris, who had been in another room, poked his head in the doorway and quipped, "We'll take it!"

We settled on a little brownstone with a large front living room window that looked onto the tree-lined street but felt as if it opened up to the entire world. You know how a place can speak to you? This room spoke to me. It said, "Kim, you're home. You're home, baby." Literally. We were across the street from St. Nicholas Park, a minute-and-a-half walk from the building where I grew up, and a five-minute walk to my grandmother's old apartment. The best part was when the owner asked a favor. There was a baby grand piano in the living room. It had been there forever, he said. Could he leave it?

Well, Chris played the piano exquisitely, any style of music, so our answer was a no-brainer—of course, the stately instrument could stay with us. Then, in asking about its history, we discovered the piano had come from the church where my mother had been baptized. We smiled at each other. It was meant to be.

Indeed, moving in also felt more blessed than stressed. As we unpacked, Chris and I needed a rental truck to move the few things he still had in storage. I had to show my driver's license to rent it, but I could not find my wallet amid all the clutter. However, while searching, I found the box with my professional memorabilia. I pulled out one of my *Jet* magazine covers. "This can be my ID," I said. Chris made no comment, but I could hear him thinking, *Is this chick serious right now?*

I was—and so were the people at the rental office. The woman in charge took the magazine, looked at me, and said, "If *Jet* says it's you, then it's you." She put keys on the counter and let us rent the van. Chris was shocked. Life in Harlem was like that, akin to a homecoming. I met my neighbors, walked in the park, and hopped on the A Train with Duke Ellington's classic song of the same name playing in my headphones. In August, I performed "HarlemHoney" from my *Smooth Is Spoken Here* album on one of the main stages at the annual Harlem Week celebration of music, art, and culture. Afterward I received a plaque that said I was their very own HarlemHoney. That was another one of those moments when you could buy me for a penny and ask for change. The move felt complete when, like every New Yorker, Chris and I found a favorite Chinese restaurant, Crispy Bamboo.

With Chris in Kansas City most of the summer, I worked on a variety of my own projects. I directed an episode of the CW series *Eve*, directed a couple concert events for BET Jazz, and played myself on the pilot of Lisa Kudrow's deeply funny and ironic HBO series *The Comeback*. Between gigs, I tapped into the New York acting community. Our close friend Lee Summers, who had written the play Chris was in, was content director for a cool little theater on West 72nd Street called The Triad, and through him I met actors, writers, and directors for coffee, talked about plays, wrote scenes, and worked on pieces together. Unlike LA, where you stayed home and waited for the phone to ring, it was easy to stay connected in New York. I loved it.

Inspired and energized, I fulfilled a dream when I launched my own clothing line, aptly named HarlemHoney. I partnered with my godmother and longtime stylist, Victoria Shaffer. The items were going to be available in an online store. I didn't know the extent of my entrepreneurial zeal until I began helping to design items (it was more casual apparel, T-shirts, shifts, and accessories than an extensive line), create the website, and work on marketing and promotional plans. I was happy with the final product and got lots of pleasure wearing my own design to Harlem Week and proudly told reporters that I was wearing me.

Here is my favorite part. Every month on the website, I wanted to spotlight a different Harlem "honey." For my inaugural pick, I shot for the moon and the stars, landing the one and only Ruby Dee. A car brought her to our apartment for a photo shoot. The fact that we had a passing acquaintance did not mitigate the awe I felt when I opened the front door and there stood Ruby Dee—writer, poet, movie star, activist, role model, legend, and American treasure.

We had corresponded several years earlier when she and her husband, Ossie Davis, had agreed to be interviewed for a documentary I wanted to do about lasting love. Then she had agreed to star in an independent movie I tried to produce. Neither of those projects came to fruition. So not until February 2005, the month before Chris and I first met, did I actually meet Ruby. It was at Riverside Church for her husband's funeral, an event that was a who's who of admirers, including former President Bill Clinton, Maya Angelou, Oprah Winfrey, Harry Belafonte, Burt Reynolds, Danny Glover, and others. I cautiously approached Ruby, who was dressed in black and wore dark sunglasses that covered half her tiny face. As I began to choose my words, she said, "Oh, you're Kim Fields. How's the movie coming?" I wrapped my arms around her and squeezed. "No, Beautiful, we're not talking about that right now. We're just lifting you up and loving on you right now."

Six months later, I was honored and a little amazed to host

her in my living room. I hoped she didn't notice that I stared at her, but she was Ruth Younger from *A Raisin in the Sun*, and beyond that, I was mesmerized by how tiny she was, yet still such a giant. I had read about such people—small in terms of height but enormous in spirit. That was Ruby Dee. I mentioned that I was still replaying Maya Angelou's words about her late husband in my head. I repeated her opening line: "The heaviest door in the universe slammed shut." I didn't have Dr. Angelou's voice or delivery, but wow, what power those words had. "That's a piece of writing I'll never forget," I said.

Later, as she waited for her car to take her home, she took a brief nap on the sofa. She was so cute. While she slept, I put the scarf I had given her as part of a gift bag of HarlemHoney goodies in our dryer to get any wrinkles out. It was warm when I folded it and placed it in her bag, and still warm when she reached in and felt it herself. "Oh, this is warm and soft, like the earth," she said. Again, I marveled at her realness and the poetry that flowed from her.

Like the earth.

Who says that?

Before leaving, she complimented our home, saying it reminded her of the Harlem she knew in its heyday. She also signed our guest book. Hers was the very first entry: *For Kim and Chris—glorious life continued in this new/old place. Ruby Dee.*

I was privileged to spend more time with her over the next few years and participate in several tributes to her. At one such tribute in Dallas, after I delivered a spoken-word piece about her, Ruby grabbed my arm and pulled me to her side. Her eyes were full of happy tears. "Oh, Kim, it's too much," she said. "It's too much." In retrospect, given that she is one of those people who inspire you to do more, and be more, it probably was not enough.

Was there a time when we didn't know you?
Didn't have you/love you/need you
Was there a time?
No. No memory of first hearing of you, seeing you
Shoot, we prayed for you to the Almighty
For a mighty wind to rush through our people
It was, is and ever shall be a surprise, your impact
'Cause we made a pact with the Almighty:
Send us an angel, we'll treat her like a Queen
Oohh, we didn't mean
To make you cry
We're sorry, Mother, for running rampant
On your one good nerve
With our killin', lyin', cheatin', beatin' selves
Takin' us backwards, after all the marchin' steps forward
    you and your beloved
took for us
Wrapping history around your finger and never letting
    go
At times choking it into submission
On your mission/journey/quest
For truth, justice, freedom . . .
There is none like you, there is no analogy
No example
You're not like anything or anyone
Comparisons are made to you
(By those who just don't know no better)
Nothing, no one compares to you
You are the measuring stick . . .
You make the oaks in your beloved South stand strong
    with pride
You make preachers want to preach
You make actors and activists want to act
You make these beings that are human want to be better

You make people of color want to be greater
You make weeping willows in your beloved South weep
    with grace
Oh let's face it,
You sho-nuff make women want to be wives
You make wives want to love better, stronger, harder,
    longer
You make humility never want to be a capital H
You HarlemHoney, are the sweet and have tasted the bit-
    ter of our beloved Harlem
You make people, couples, want a love like yours
The Greatest Love Story Ever Told...
Oh, do I bring this up? How can I not bring this up?:
We ached for you
You were our first and only thought that awful February
    day
We had not ached like that
Perhaps since '63, '65, or '68
For Jacqueline, Betty, and Coretta
For you we ached...
Now, hear with ears as open as your heart
Here is my heart
So full, thoughts so scattered
Assaulted and battered by love for you
Knocked off my feet
Overwhelmed with connection
Yearning for direction
To place this love, respect, admiration, illumination
Ah yes, light does come from deep within you
Finding its way to me
Believe, I know others feel it too,
But I'm greedy and selfish when it comes to you
You've touched me
Though I'm not yet even born, you've reached me

Beyond the womb, into the universe
This verse is for you who has touched me
Reached me, taken hold of me with your
Voice, integrity, mastery of art/word/prose
I suppose I wish to be, long to be... Because you have
    been
I have a spirit, your spirit
Though I don't even have life yet
Not yet formed
But already formed by you because you touched me
Reaching across space and time
Not God-like
Yet not unlike God
Surely you and the Almighty must be tight, right?
Nothing but a Holy hand could implant such
Talent, beauty and compassion
Beautiful, enduring
Strong as granite, granted, that's a surface
And the last thing you are is surface
No, Mother, you are deep, deep and lovely
Like... Like...
Now didn't I say there's no analogy, no example, no
    measuring stick?
The Nile and Euphrates are as deep and lovely as Ms.
    Ruby
Ruby—I will not give in to the notion to plunge into an
    ocean of phrases
paralleling your name and gems, precious stones
I will with stone face receive the notion to plunge into an
    ocean of witty weaving of
Character names you've donned,
Awards and honors given since the dawning of your ca-
    reer hitting its stride
But ooooohhhhh the pride, the pride Mother I feel

When I think of the goodness of Ossie and Ruby and all
   they've done for me my
soul cries out Hallelujah!!!!!
No disrespect, no blasphemin'
But it is spiritual
You know they have been kissed on the forehead by the
   Almighty
Right here, in the center, in the sweet-spot
Where only the one who loves you mercifully, gracefully
   and sweetly can
The same way, Mother, you love
your beloved and your children and your grandchildren
   and your people
From one HarlemHoney to another,
I will always be on full
When it comes to Ms. Ruby Dee
When it comes to you.

For Chris and me, living together in these early days was
more of a series of reunions. After he finished *From My Home
Town*, he started *Once on This Island* in Baltimore. I spent
March and April 2006 on the road in the gospel-themed play
Issues: We All Got 'Em. Fortunately, the two of us were extremely compatible when we were home together. We loved
being in our backyard (a rare and coveted slice of real estate
in NYC), which we named Kismet. We enjoyed going to the
theater, hanging out in local restaurants, working on our craft,
talking about acting, and having friends over. When we did hit
those cohabitating speed bumps, we talked—more often than I
was used to in relationships.

But Chris was more complex and evolved than most of the
men I had encountered in my life—and maybe most men in
general. He had studied psychology and communications at
James Madison University. He was in touch with his feelings

and shared them with me, and when he was done sharing, he wanted to know how I was feeling, and after that, we explored what those feelings meant and how they connected to the other feelings. Not usually my style of communication. I cherry-picked what I wanted to bring to the table. I kept things inside me—sometimes forever or sometimes until I could no longer contain them and probably uncork. Not the best way to navigate through difficult or challenging moments, I know, but I don't like conflict. In general, I did not like to rock the boat. Chris was the opposite— not in terms of rocking the boat, but in wanting to ensure it sailed as smooth and efficiently as possible, which meant we needed more frequent *dialogues*, not him sharing and me saying, "Okay, gotcha."

We were both trying to bring the wisdom and lessons learned from our previous marriages and relationships. Wisdom and learning, not baggage. One day, we were in the midst of some conversation, going round and round, when I put my hands on my hips and said, "You know, it seems like you're giving a lot of notes at the start of rehearsal. You haven't even seen what I can do and you've given me notes." After a long pause, he laughed and then we both laughed together—and at each other. It was good.

In all transparency, over the decade we've been married and nearly thirteen years we've been together, I'm still working on some of the basic tenets of love and marriage. Understanding that while there are some things that work as Wife, I have to be clear and nonjudgmental about what works as Chris's wife...what lands with him. And vice versa. One of our best talks was late one evening, under a cool, moonlit night. He said, "Baby, I see you're working hard for us, for me. I see your efforts, they're just not in the right direction." It made me think of the time I celebrated my eighteenth birthday in San Diego and was driving (rushing) to the airport. I knew the airport was south. The issue was, it was not south of where I was at the time, the zoo. Imagine my frustration and surprise when I started seeing signs that welcomed me to Tijuana.

As for my initiating potentially difficult communication, someone once told me, "The Word says 'blessed are the peacemakers'...makers, not peace keepers. Think of all the great peacemakers and what they went through. To make peace, sometimes takes uncomfortable work." I'm not where I may need to be, but I'm not where I used to be on that.

Another lesson: Don't judge whatever language your spouse speaks in love. If someone speaks a foreign language and you are engaging with them, you work on learning how to speak to them and vice versa. However, reluctantly learning is not cool; that does not make them feel like you want to talk to them. Nor is getting aggravated or judging why they speak the language they do. They just do, same as you. That was a revelation in the early days in the Morgan home.

In the summer of 2006, we solved the issue of being apart so frequently. We worked on a project together. BET Jazz approached me about creating, producing, and directing three and a half hours of programming for a partnership they had with Royal Caribbean Cruises. I created a three-part *Love Boat*–inspired miniseries. Titled *A Royal Birthday*, it was about a handful of girlfriends who go on a cruise for a joint celebration and end up on a journey of self-discovery and romance.

I hired Chris as one of the male leads. We shot on two separate cruises, which was an added delight, and on the two days off between the two cruises, as Chris and I were heading home on the train, he looked at me and said, "I'm ready to start our family." I burst into tears—happy tears—right there.

I had no concerns of starting a family in my late thirties. I was healthy and relatively fit. I trusted the Lord and modern medicine to do everything they could to make sure the baby and I were healthy. Apparently my body was also down with the program because Chris and I had only started to try to get pregnant when I came out of the bathroom one morning with the little magic wand in my hand. Chris was not even able to ask if what I was holding was what he thought it was before I said simply, "Yup, it is. And we are."

I was exhausted through my first trimester. Chris was working on a play just north of the city, in Westchester County, and I couldn't stand when he would come back home after a long day of rehearsing or an exhausting performance and an hour train ride to find me in the same spot on the couch I was in when he left, wiped out. But he comforted me, saying things like, "Don't be so hard on yourself. Do you realize you probably made a kneecap today?"

My family was excited. This was the first grandchild, so they were over the moon. Chris's older sister already had children, but his parents were still overjoyed, of course. As my pregnancy progressed, my energy returned. I went to the gym, swam, and worked with one of Chris's best friends, a personal trainer, who guided me through prenatal training. My pregnancy was a joy. In November, I appeared in the long-running play *Speak Truth to Power*, Ariel Dorfman's moving adaptation of Kerry Kennedy's book on people who have fought for human rights and social justice. Chris and I spent Christmas with his parents in Richmond.

By January, Chris and I were desperate to find out the sex of the new life growing in me. "Please tell us who's in there," I pleaded with my doctor at the next checkup. Chris echoed my request. Both of us were convinced we were having a girl. Chris's sister had a daughter. I came from a family of girls. My mom had one sister, and her mother came from thirteen sisters. By the time the doctor had a picture of my belly up on her monitor, Chris and I were running down our potential girl names— that is, until the doctor said, "Not so fast."

I turned my head. "Is everything okay?"

The doctor nodded. "There's the heartbeat. It looks good. And right there is the evidence that you are having a boy."

I was thrilled, shocked, amazed, and overjoyed. I squeezed Chris's hand. "Oh my God," I said. "A boy. Thank You, Lord."

* * *

With my face still wet from all the happy tears I'd cried in the doctor's office, I called my parents with the good news. Chris phoned his parents, too. Both of our mothers spoke to me about the special love a son has for his mom and the protection he will always provide. I was overwhelmed with the profundity of creating this life that would help replenish the earth with a beautiful, smart, strong black man. So many of our men had been senselessly, violently taken from us, and here was my contribution to reversing that fact. I was not at that place where I thought about what he might do in life. It was just the fact that he would be, period.

Chris loved the name Sebastian. As a boy, one of his favorite movies was *The NeverEnding Story*, in which the lead boy's name was Bastian. We thought Sebastian Morgan was quite a name and perhaps he'd need a nickname in school, so we gave him the middle initial A to create the nickname SAM. Sebastian Alexander Morgan. Of course, no one uses it.

In the middle months of my pregnancy, I toured for the second time in the play *Issues: We All Got 'Em*. Chris and my sister, Alexis, were also in it, ensuring every performance was a family affair. On the road, we fell into a daily routine of waking, eating, walking, resting, performing, and chilling. I listened to my friend Maxwell's "Urban Hang Suite," which filled me and my unborn son with peace and beauty. At 4:00 p.m., he began to stir, as if aware I was heading to the theater. At 8:00 p.m., he heard the overture and knew the play was about to start and began to move, as if limbering up. "Time to calm down," Chris would say to my tummy. "Sebastian, Mommy needs you to be calm for a little bit." And if we had a day off, Sebastian would still stir in the afternoon, as if to say, "Hey, aren't we supposed to be going to the theater now?"

Navigating pregnancy, work, and traveling didn't leave much room for anything else, which was a bit frustrating to handle when the presidential campaign for Barack Obama began to ramp up. Everything in me wanted to be a part of the campaign and movement. Especially when I had a very brief hello and handshake with Senator Obama at JFK airport. Aside from pledging my support to him and an aide (in passing), I wouldn't get the chance to do more than make financial contributions and cast my vote for him. I remember telling Chris that night, "Guess who I saw at the airport? Barack Obama! He was nice!"

We also traveled to Las Vegas for the annual Trumpet Awards, where I announced to the who's who of the community, including CeCe Winans, Usher, Toni Braxton, and Kenny "Babyface" Edmonds, that I was having a boy and he was going to become someone we all were proud of. At the reception, it seemed as if everyone in attendance touched my belly and shared in our happiness.

We finished the night dancing at a super-private, super-intimate performance by Prince at his 3121 club. We could almost reach out and touch him. Of course, he was amazing—and so was Sebastian, who felt like he danced the whole time in my belly, especially when the Purple One closed his show with "Let's Go Crazy."

Speaking of crazy, that is what my doctor called me when I said I wanted to have a water birth at home. "Not at thirty-eight, you aren't," she said. My due date was my birthday, May 12. We scheduled a C-section the week before, on May 4, and planned to welcome him into the world with a soundtrack of favorite songs playing in the background. Chris and I put together a special Birthing Room Playlist that included "Family" from *Dreamgirls* and Cassandra Wilson's "Someday My Prince Will Come." Each song was carefully and lovingly selected.

Once in the birthing room, though, we realized we had forgotten our iPod back in our room. The anesthesiologist told Chris and me to relax. "I'll sing with you," he said, and the three of us sang our songs and harmonized as the doctor gently said, "Okay, now you're going to feel a big push, like I'm pressing down on you. Just a little pressure . . . Sebastian, I'm coming to get you . . . and . . ."

A moment later, I was handed this cute little bundle of perfection. He weighed six pounds and change, and his eyes looked wide open and alert as he heard his name, for the first time. "Hello, Sebastian," I said. "We love you." Our families felt the same way. Both sides poured into my hospital room to see our prince. Less than a week later, it was time to take Sebastian home. My parents and our friend performer-writer-teacher-remarkable human being Q. Smith, were there. Chris rented a minivan and drove about three miles per hour. "Has Chris ever driven before?" my mother jokingly asked me. "Yes, he has," Chris chimed in. "But this is precious cargo."

From the first late-night feeding, I knew motherhood was my favorite role ever. I remember sitting up late with Sebastian, staring at him as he ate, counting his fingers, pinching his toes, and loving him more deeply than I'd imagined possible. Chris was working locally, so he gave Sebastian a bottle before going to work and let me sleep in. I spent my days like other new mothers. I read all the popular baby books, pushed Sebastian through my beloved St. Nicholas Park, the same park where I had played as a little girl. "That's where Mommy used to run and jump and swing," I'd say. That blew me away.

One day my sisterfriend Lalah Hathaway sent me a text that said, "Kirk is looking for you." So I texted Kirk Franklin. "Hey, bro, you looking for me?"

He said, "No, but nice hearing from you." Lalah then clarified: It was musician Kirk Whalum who wanted to speak with me. It turned out the brilliant saxophonist had heard my spoken word and wanted to collaborate. "I'll send you a track," he said. "Do your thing and I'll play around with whatever you come up with."

Stunned and flattered, I listened to his track while I did Sebastian's overnight feedings. His dreamy jazz matched my half-awake, half-asleep state of mind and gradually lyrics came to me until I wrote the piece "In a Whisper." Kirk put the track on what would become his Grammy-nominated album *Round Trip*. I still remember one reviewer said of our track, "It's hot." I was good with that.

Later that summer, life had settled into a mostly predictable routine. One day, while pushing my napping baby through the park, I was hit with all that had happened since moving back to Harlem. In just two years, I had gone from asking Chris how we could live in the same zip code to caring for our two-month-old. By His grace, we had created a rich life for ourselves in New York City. My old hometown had become my new hometown. New friends were like old friends.

One night we were sitting on our bed, planning the next few months of work and travel. Chris mentioned wanting to give Los Angeles a try after his upcoming gig in Oklahoma City. A few of his friends had moved west to see if they could transition to TV and film from the stage. I said, "All right. I hear you. But what's the immediate plan?"

It was a loaded question. As Chris knew from previous discussions, I was gun-shy about moving to LA. It would change the relatively stable world we'd created in New York. I feared revisiting the dialogue from my first marriage when I heard of a change in the plan. Chris had a huge career in regional theater and Broadway. Hearing him want to reinvent himself for Hollywood didn't quite feel like what I'd signed on for. I'd felt like I'd just left LA. I wasn't interested in going back. But again, I wasn't going to be anybody's dream killer, especially this talented man's. So we talked goals and plans. We moved slowly. I was going to be with Christopher Morgan for the long haul, so this time around I wanted to bring wisdom, not baggage.

On July 23, we called my old friend Pastor Donnie McClurkin, and later that afternoon we were standing in his office, exchanging I Do's. It was raining like crazy, and Donnie's church was way out on Long Island. We took a train, a cab, a yak...It took forever to get out there, which was a good metaphor for marriage: There will be bumps and obstacles, but you don't give up; you don't get out of the car. You laugh through difficulties, and you make sure there's a touch of magic.

We were met there by another longtime family friend, Louis Mellini—yup, my prom chauffeur, surrogate big brother, and Donnie's brother-in-law. He was our witness. Knowing I'd take at least one photo, I wore a nice orange dress and a head scarf. But that was it for formalities. Midway through the ceremony, we paused to change Sebastian's diaper. When we started up again, Donnie asked for the rings. Both Chris and I traded looks of panic. We'd forgotten them.

Thinking quickly, Chris went over to Donnie's desk, found gold paper clips, and quickly fashioned two of them into rings—one of which he put on his finger and the other one on mine. "I do," he said.

"I do," I said. "Forever."

And yes, we still have our gold paper clip rings.

19

Mother

Iam in awe of my husband's talent. Truly, as I mentioned earlier, he takes my breath away when he performs. Some of the biggest goose bumps of my life have come while watching him perform onstage. The look on his face when he takes his bow in front of an audience comes from deep inside his soul. It is the picture of someone who is doing exactly what he should be doing at that moment in time. I believe that's another reason why I was hesitant about moving to LA. Casting in the film and TV business is often about the bigger, better thing, not the most talented person in the room, and I did not want to see my husband's brilliance tarnished in any way.

I was being protective of both of us, I suppose. I didn't want him to be hurt, and I didn't want us to suffer. But Chris was passionate. He was at an age where he wanted to try. He knew it was a risk, but he felt like he had to take it.

As much as I had always feared this sort of life, one without a safety net, I loved this man too much to say anything but, "I support you, Mr. Morgan."

I had only one condition: I wanted to keep our place in Harlem. Once all that was straightened out, we made a plan and headed west. I wish I could say that everything worked out the way we wanted. Unfortunately, Chris had an extremely difficult time. Despite twenty-plus years of experience, he had to reestablish himself. It was like starting from scratch, which he was prepared to do, but when you are a thirty-year-old man with skills that put you at the top of your craft and no one cares, or they tell you directly that your skills are not enough and that your resume doesn't matter, it's painful.

And for both of us. I hated to see him hurt and suffering. It put a terrible stress on our marriage. The challenging times often felt like they would eat us alive, but we held on to each other and hung in there. Finding a church home helped tremendously, not only with caring for our spirit but also with providing an outlet for Chris, who thrived in the music department. We also had (and will always have) our humor . . .

One day Chris came home to find me ecstatic about an audition I'd just been called in for. I was running around getting my look together, which included my knee-high white leather go-go boots. The role was for Storm in X-Men. I kept saying how surprised I was Halle was no longer doing the fantastic mutant superhero, but okay, I'm in! I was working on my scene in my outfit when I read the info more carefully and it hit me like a ton of bricks: My audition was for the animated series. This was a voice-over audition. Halle wasn't goin' nowhere. When I tell you, Chris and I to this very day laugh our butts off heartily, doubled over, screaming with laughter at that one.

Writing became my outlet, my lifeline to calm and sanity. I wrote a one-woman play titled *Black Don't Crack, but My Soul Does Ache*. It was a collection of character sketches, different people inside me clamoring to get out. Through them, I unloaded my opinions on life, love, work, and social issues; deeply cathartic, it was like a year of therapy.

I also began writing for practical reasons. I didn't want to wait for someone to hire me. I didn't want to audition and then wonder if they liked me. So I put pen to paper and created a job for myself. I wanted to act. I wanted to stretch as an artist and dig deep inside myself—and that's exactly what I did. Chris booked a wonderful gig at the Hollywood Bowl, a production of *Guys & Dolls*. It had a fantastic cast featuring the incomparable Brian Stokes Mitchell (whom I had a teen crush on from when he was on the TV series *Trapper John, M.D.*—I even had an autographed picture of him in my dressing room) and the lovely Jessica Biel. It was a marvelous boost for Chris. And as always, he took my breath away.

In February 2009, I premiered *Black Don't Crack* at a friend's theater in Dallas. Chris, who helped me come up with an ending for the show, was there with Sebastian. Lisa Whelchel also came to one performance. The audiences ate it up, enthusiastically connecting with the material with shouts of "Preach" and "Yes, ma'am" and "Amen." It was everything I'd hoped and more.

I believe you create your own breaks, sometimes for no other reason than to keep your mind occupied, as was the case with my play. At the same time, I knew that God was creating alongside me. I called it a one-woman show, but it wasn't a solo project. He had guided me through everything I'd been through and given me the gifts of being able to write and produce. To that end, the play seemed to put a positive energy into the world that opened new doors for me. One day I got a call from my mom, who said that I was going to get a call from Tyler Perry's people. Tyler had begun producing, writing, and directing TV shows for TBS in Atlanta, including *House of Payne*. He was also about to launch *Meet the Browns*.

With a workload that also included movies, he had started to look for other directors to help with his TV series and he called my mom, whom he's always loved. Luckily for me, Chip was busy. She said something like, "Oh, I'm not flying back and forth right now. You should call Kimmy."

My mom is like that—a generous spirit. If she can't do a job, she recommends who she feels is the next best person. As a result, I heard from Tyler's right-hand man and executive producer Roger Bobb, who met with me at a restaurant on Sunset Boulevard. We had a great talk and before I knew it, they flew me, Chris, and Sebastian to Atlanta for a couple days so I could observe the way they worked in preparation to direct an episode of my own.

I will never forget that first day I walked into Tyler Perry Studios—actually, forget walking in; just arriving there and standing in front of the gates gave me chills. I looked at his name and was so proud of this person and all that he had overcome. I had met Tyler years before and experienced the brightness of his smile and the force of his eyes when talking to him. The man radiated an energy that was unparalleled. He had seen me in a production of *Barefoot in the Park* at the National Black Theater Festival and also that night discovered a friend of mine I had put in the play, Cassi Davis, who he then used in several of his projects, including *House of Payne*.

Tyler's world was something else. You do not simply carve out your own place in the entertainment industry and build a studio with your name on the gates. The people who did this were named Warner and Mayer and Goldwyn. Oprah had Harpo Studios in Chicago but had not yet launched OWN, her own network. So as I walked in, I took in the fact that somebody had done this. Then add that this somebody was once homeless. And this somebody was abused. And oh yeah, this somebody is a black man.

But those were not my points of entry for admiring Tyler Perry. No, the thing that impressed me most was the thing that got him to this place. He was, quite simply, exceptional.

When I got to the set of *Meet the Browns*, Tyler jumped right into rehearsal. It was a hug and a kiss and "let's go." As Roger had explained, Tyler's method of making TV was different than the traditional way shows were produced. Indeed, Tyler did everything at his own pace, which was fast; he shot one show a day compared to one show a week. I shadowed him for a few days/episodes and then at the end of the third he said, "Okay, Kimmy, tomorrow you're up."

Tyler was and is a complete and utter visionary. He is highly creative and full of enthusiasm and love for what he does. He knows every character and every story line of every one of his movies and TV shows. He knows his audience—what they like, what they do not like, what they will react to. He knows the lane he has created. He is focused, but also playful and a world-class multitasker. He can operate brilliantly in several playgrounds at the same time.

When my turn came, I brought my A-game, as I knew I had to. I got the script and ran everyone through their blocking for cameras. My efforts got a thumbs-up from the maestro and I kept going. Once we knew the work was going to be a real gig rather than a two-week trial, they moved us from the hotel to a beautiful condo in midtown Atlanta. A short time later, I turned forty years old. Tyler sent flowers and the show's cast helped me celebrate with a large birthday cake. That night, Chris and I went to the movies, as was our tradition on my birthday.

But forty.

Wow.

I reacted by cutting my locks. Cliché? Maybe. But I felt like a new level of womanhood was supposed to begin. The problem was, I did not have a vision of what that was for me. I just knew it was supposed to look different, and so, after a decade of my blond locks, my boho glam, it was snip-snip-snip. But there were changes beyond a new do that began to define this new chapter for me. For instance, we moved. After the season ended, we returned to Los Angeles, packed up everything, put some stuff in storage, and created a new home in Atlanta.

In 2010, Chris starred in a touring company of *Ain't Misbehavin'*. At home, I drove Sebastian to preschool and then went to the set. We used Skype and FaceTime to stay in contact multiple times a day and visited Chris in San Jose and Phoenix. It was not a traditional life, but it was the life of two working, adult performers. On the plane, as Sebastian played with toys, I leaned back in my chair, one of those rare mommy breaks when I had time to take a deep breath and reflect.

I was so proud of Chris and happy to see his spirit soaring again. He was so present in Sebastian's early years, it was a blessing to be able to say to him, "Baby, definitely go and take wings." I was grateful that God provided the opportunity to remind Chris that He still had his back, that He still knew what was in Chris's heart and created the fire in his belly. As for me, I thought, *Okay, this is who we are. This is what we do. This is how we support each other. We create balance—whatever that means.*

It meant Chris had a great run in *Ain't Misbehavin'*. I was directing *Meet the Browns*. We had a lovely home in the burbs. Sebastian and I were in a great routine. He loved preschool. We were good.

* * *

"How is it down there?" My mom was calling from California. Tyler's first choice to direct before I got the job, she was headed to Atlanta to direct episodes of his other TV series, *House of Payne*. If I am not mistaken, we are the only mother-daughter team to direct network television, let alone do it simultaneously, but that is what happened. Both of us were helming shows for Tyler Perry. There was no time to hang out, even though our soundstages were next door to each other, but my mom's inspiring vibe permeated the walls and I grooved on knowing she was nearby.

Outside of work, she was able to spend time with her grandson. Sebastian was still a little guy and loved spending time with 'MomMom' on the weekends. Back in LA, my sister, Alexis, was raising her own child. About a year and a half after Sebastian was born, she and her husband had the first of their two children, a baby girl named Kaycie. The day Alexis got married and then later brought that sweet treat into the world, she went from being my little sister and one of my best girlfriends to one of my best girlfriends and a woman I admired.

I was content with my life in A-Town, but not so content that I quit hustling. I knew how the world worked, especially the show business world, and I knew it was best to have something waiting in the wings. Chris and I created *Holiday Love*, the first of what has turned out to be an annual TV special modeled after the family-friendly variety shows I remembered fondly from my childhood. Filled with stars and music and funny skits, it was like Andy Williams's Christmas specials. It ran on TV One on Christmas Eve as a lead-in to a Beyoncé special and was encored on Christmas day.

The following year TV One aired *Holiday Love* at 7:00 a.m. Christmas morning. Boy, was I was mad. I was like, "You know the show. You know it did well last year. I expanded it to two hours. You know I'm working my butt off to promote it. Why do you put it on Christmas morning?"

Chris talked me down. "Baby, something's better than nothing," he said.

Okay. Heeding the advice of my sage husband, I spun my frustration into a positive: "TV One has your first Christmas gift. It's *Holiday Love*." I envisioned growing this as a brand—and we did. We have continued it one way or another via syndication and in the digital space with our online channel as well as an annual radio special with over a million listeners. In

November, Chris joined the cast of *Ghost Brothers of Darkland County*, a new Southern gothic musical from author Stephen King and rocker John Mellencamp. Workshops began at the Alliance Theater in December and performances, which began with a world premiere in April 2012, were sold out immediately.

By then, Chris and I had another production in the works. We were going to have a baby. We did not tell anyone outside of our families; it was too soon. In May, our dreams were put on hold when we suffered a miscarriage. There was no horrific drama or visuals. As I like to say, there was mercy involved. It happened over a period that spanned my birthday and Mother's Day in 2012, which also happened to be the weekend Chris's play ended its run at the Alliance. The hospital staff was incredible. When they realized it was my birthday and Mother's Day, they gave me cards for both, doing their best to lift my spirits even a little bit.

Perhaps not coincidentally, I had recently read Charles Swindoll's profile of David and, in particular, the section where he wrote about the miscarriage David and Bathsheba had before Solomon was born. Their child was conceived in a very different way—obviously our circumstances were very different—but I'd noted the way they handled it and then a few weeks later, following our miscarriage, I said to myself, "Wait a minute. Didn't I just read something similar?"

It was information that had been put there for me to use at a later date, as God does all the time. Likewise my husband was a pillar of strength and comfort. I could lean on him or curl up next to him and get the love I needed at that vulnerable moment. He never once said, "She had a miscarriage" or "She lost the baby." It was always about us. "We suffered a miscarriage," he said. Or "We are getting through it."

Afterward, I healed the best way I knew, by working. I had booked a part on the movie *What to Expect When You're Expect-*

ing, the Jennifer Lopez comedy based on the bestselling book that has been every expectant woman's guide through pregnancy, including me. I auditioned and got to work with Jennifer and Roberto Santiago as the social worker who helped with their adoption. The book's author, Heidi Murkoff, signed the copy I'd had on my shelf since I was pregnant with Sebastian. I confided what had just happened to me and Chris. "It will work out for you," she said.

We had doubts when we suffered a second miscarriage right before New Year's Day. At my regular checkup, Chris and I and were told the baby's heartbeat was weak. We left her office knowing all we could do was pray, and that's what we did, as did everyone in our family. However, on New Year's, we lost the baby. On the way to the hospital, I turned to Chris and said, "Another miscarriage on a holiday? Really? If it has to happen, why can't it just be Tuesday, August 20—or something random?" The nursing staff was so sorry to see us under these circumstances again. I remember a nurse walking into my room and saying, "Oh, hell no, not you two again—and of all the days." Their outpouring of love brought tears to my eyes.

The anesthesia preceding the D&C (dilation and curettage) brought another reaction. As I sat in my bed, I started to scream (as if I was grooving to music in my head), "Quincy Jones! Emerald City!" I hollered it at the top of my lungs, like I was in a club. "Quincy Jones! Emerald City!" Chris cracked up. "You are so high," he said.

Yeah.

But.

"Quincy Jones! Emerald City!"

* * *

Chris and I told only our family and closest friends about both miscarriages. Not many people knew I had been pregnant. After

I sent out the email, the responses came back instantly. The phone also rang nonstop for days. We were blown away by the number of people who said, "Guys, this happened to us, too. You're going to be okay." We never knew. Then, suddenly, we were all sharing. It was like going to some bizarre speakeasy you never knew existed. But once down there and your eyes adjust to the darkness, it's like, "Oh crap, you're here, too?"

After a D&C, the doctor gives you a window of time to heal from the procedure. Toward the end of that window, Chris and I were intimate. Afterward, we were concerned. "Did we mess up by not waiting the exact number of days?" I wondered. But I seemed fine and we went on with our lives. It was April, and there was a flu going around. Sebastian came home from school sick. Then I got really sick. I thought I had the same thing, but Chris said, "No, babe, you seem sicker than Sebastian," and took me to the doctor.

On the way, I decided I was premenopausal rather than sick. I had been writing and researching for a script and wanted one of the characters to be premenopausal, so I knew all the symptoms and self-diagnosed myself. It made me angry. "Are you kidding me?" I exclaimed to God in the car. "Are you kidding me? First two miscarriages. Then menopause. Come on, Jesus, this is so uncool."

I was still ranting when the doctor came into the examining room. By this time, I was a wreck. I told her my symptoms as well as the diagnosis. "I'm premenopausal," I said. "And it's just horrible." Because the doctor had been our doctor since we moved to Atlanta, she knew my credentials as a diagnostician were from the University of I Looked It Up on Google, and so she did a full workup on me, including a blood test. After a short wait, she came back into the room and said, "You are two months pregnant." I was stunned. "What? What do you mean I'm pregnant?"

I looked for Chris before remembering he was waiting in the car with Sebastian, who had fallen asleep. I pulled out my cell phone and called him. "I got something to tell you," I said. "I'll be right there." I got in the car, shut the door, and put my face right up in his. "I'm pregnant," I said. He leaned back and very slowly every pore in his body turned into a gigantic smile. "I told you that you were sicker than Sebastian," he said. "I told you that you were sick."

After that initial bout of sickness, my pregnancy was smooth sailing. Though I was forty-four years old, my doctor did not prescribe rest or recommend anything out of the ordinary. "You feel good," she said. "Do your thing." Unlike my first pregnancy, though, I developed a mad craving for cereal. We could not keep it in the house. Our pantry looked like the breakfast aisle at the grocery store—Cap'n Crunch, Corn Pops, and Cocoa Krispies. Sebastian, who thought I was still pregnant from the first time, was thrilled when we told him that he was going to have a little brother.

I told the rest of the world our good news on the TV talk show *The Real*. I know, I know, it was not the most traditional way to let the world know I was eating for two. At the end of July 2013, I went on and announced I was having my second boy as well as the fact that Chris and I had already picked out a name, one I'd loved for years, Quincy Xavier.

My fans left the most incredible reactions on social media. "She looks amazing," one woman wrote. "I hope I still have my own face when I get pregnant." Another person said, "She still looks fine as hell." And still another said, "Black don't crack! She's beautiful." As I went into my ninth month, I was of course heavier than normal, but I felt strong enough to shoot our latest *Holiday Love* special, which was titled *The Rebirth*. Afterward, I converted half our kitchen into an editing suite—my idea of being barefoot and pregnant in the kitchen.

As for the birth itself, I had another elective C-section. The little fella arrived at 10:30 in the morning on December 3, weighing slightly more than eight pounds. As with Sebastian, tears filled my eyes as the nurse laid him down on my chest. Chris kissed both of us and announced the baby was here and healthy to both sets of our parents who were waiting outside for the news. Despite the painkillers I had been given, I spent the afternoon negotiating a distribution deal for *Holiday Love: The Rebirth* from my bed. Hey, I wore two hats—mom and mogul.

"He is a blessing," I told Chris's parents before turning to my mom and adding, "and so is our distribution deal." Within two weeks, we were back home and in our routines. Both of our parents had left and I was doing press for *Holiday Love* when Sebastian came down with a mystery illness. He ran a fever at night and it spiked the next morning. Also, he couldn't move his legs.

Chris carried Sebastian downstairs while I bundled up Quincy and we drove to the doctor, figuring she would make a diagnosis and prescribe some medicine. We told Sebastian that we'd pick up a Christmas tree afterward, hoping that would boost his spirits. Instead the doctor looked at Sebastian and ordered us straight to the children's hospital. I felt like I was in the twilight zone as I watched a doctor examine our six-year-old and then tell me his enzymes were 200 percent higher than they should be and although he didn't have blood in his urine he was going to be admitted. "He was running around two days ago," I said. "Then this morning he couldn't walk. What's going on?"

What was going on was rhabdomyolysis, a breakdown of muscles that can lead to kidney damage. Determined not to get distracted with fear (or the sheer wonder of what caused this), Chris and I stayed focused on our faith, our children, and each other. Barely two weeks old, Quincy was not allowed in the hospital, so we traded shifts being with each child. Chris slept at the hospital one night and I slept there the next. At night, I read the cards Sebastian's classmates from school had sent, talked to friends, and walked the halls. I flashed back to when I was twelve and had been rushed to a children's hospital for an emergency appendectomy. I realized my mom had walked similar halls on the other side of the country, worrying about me. I asked her what she did while I was in surgery. "I prayed," she said.

I prayed, too. For four days, Sebastian was given fluids until his entire system had been flushed out. As his enzyme count returned to normal, he did, too. I knew he was his normal self when he asked if could have a hamburger and French fries for dinner and go back to school.

After checking Sebastian out of the hospital, we stopped at our regular Christmas tree lot, thankful to see the owners, the Cooks, and basking in their wonderful smiles, hugs, and spirit. The familiar smell of the trees and fire pit was a welcome return to our norm after a week of anything but. We bought the biggest Christmas tree we could strap to the car, possibly a bit of an outward expression of the enormous amount of gratitude we felt for the extraordinary blessings of life and health. "Mommy, we can put Quincy under the tree this year," Sebastian said. "He's like a little present." That stopped me in my tracks. I reached out and hugged my boy so hard he had to wriggle out to take a breath. "Baby, both of you are the most precious gifts we could ever have." He looked at me as only a six-year-old boy can when things do not make sense. "But you can't put me under the tree. I'm too big to fit in a box."

He was back—and so was I. Talk about miracles. But people have the capacity to bounce back, especially children. As for my own resilience, it must be God-given because if it were up to me, I would not be that way. But I cannot go crazy. No one is going to read about me in the middle of the street, half naked, with my hair all over my head, screaming—as much as I would like to sometimes. Not with all the work, tears, and prayers everyone in my village has given me. That is not what my mother signed on for. That is not what my village signed on for. My resilience is such that I can take a lot and I can let a lot roll off me. Then, when I do succumb, it is quick. I do not live there. I deal with my pain, acknowledge my pain, allow myself to feel it, and then I get on with the healing and the learning and the living.

"Be anxious for nothing, but in all things give thanks" (Philippians 4:6). Embracing that line of Scripture, one of my favorites, eliminates some of the stress in our modern lives—and also some of the worry lines that can show up on your face. Hey, even though black don't crack, who needs to take the risk?

20

#TrueToMyself

With two children, the reality of my life turned me into a master juggler of schedules. Our kitchen had a multi-layered, color-coded calendar: one for Chris's life; one for my life; one for Sebastian's school, which included projects and homework; and one for Quincy's checkups and playdates. I had days that I am sure every mom can relate to when I felt more like an executive secretary than any of the other jobs on my resume. My life skills now included changing a diaper while in the drive-through lane at Chick-fil-A and doing conference calls with agents and producers in Hollywood while I made dinner, checked second-grade math problems, and listened for any peeps coming from the baby monitor.

So I welcomed the chance to shoot the Hallmark movie *For Better or for Worse* with my lifelong friend Lisa Whelchel in Vancouver. Sebastian had rolled with us on locations from infancy and that work-life lifestyle (yeah, I don't call it *balance*) continued with two wonderful kids in tow. This charming coastal city opened its welcoming arms as I checked into the hotel with two little boys and one of our sitters. Thankfully, production was over Sebastian's spring break and I enrolled him in camp at the fabulous aquarium there. Both boys visited the set, too. Alexis was also able to break away for a couple days to spend time with the boys. As always, we were a Gypsy-esque family ever grateful for FaceTime and Skype.

One day Lisa and her daughter taught Sebastian how to play Uno. He referred to her as Aunty Lisa, and her children, who were older, had always known me as Aunt Kim. These were some of the joys of a long friendship. I found it slightly surreal, though, to be working with Lisa again at this stage of our lives. I was trying to get comfortable in my post-baby skin, and she had gotten divorced two years earlier. She confided that she was thinking about trying to date again, but did not exactly know how to do it in this age of dating apps. It reminded me of when I had called Nancy to ask how to shave my legs. Except here Lisa and I were, she at age fifty-one and me still the kid sis at forty-five, trying to figure it all out.

The movie aired in July and I remember a *People* magazine reporter saying it was good to see that Lisa and I were not screwed up like other former child actors from the '80s. Lisa and I said, "Of course we aren't." We had strong families, good friendships, and old-fashioned values, including hard work and, of course, our faith.

In other words, I was sane (with a splash of normal and a dash of artsy), which, by Hollywood standards, made me...borderline uninteresting personally.

It was the reason I was mystified every time my longtime manager and friend, Art Rutter, called with an offer for a reality series. My life was acting, directing, speaking engagements, an occasional red carpet appearance, driving in school carpools, and pushing a cart up and down the aisles at my local Publix Super Market. Was that interesting? But the calls came in. At one point Chris and I said yes to a production company. They came to the house a few days before my C-section with Quincy and shot some test footage. It wasn't like they put cameras strategically around the house and let us live our lives, then edited what the cameras captured. They navigated and created moments from our lifestyle, making the experience a bit more intrusive than we would have liked. Padding through our kitchen, I felt enormous, like I imagined a blue whale felt at the end of her gestation period. If the sizzle presentation they put together didn't sell, we decided we would say no to reality offers and focus on our busy careers and raising two little boys.

I can't say I was disappointed. I understood why producers and networks were enamored with reality shows. They are relatively inexpensive to make, they get ratings, and they generate buzz. As an actor, though, when reality shows first hit the scene, I thought they clogged the pipes and took spots on network schedules that would've otherwise gone to scripted dramas and comedies and employed talented performers as opposed to outrageous personalities. My heroes were people who tried to elevate the human condition and inspire people. With very few exceptions, reality TV seemed to do the opposite. It mostly showed people at their worst. But the genre had created and grown an audience, and it was here to stay. Networks have been created for it, making room again for scripted projects to come home. In addition, the digital spaces created wonderful outlets for the scripted world.

I was with my kids in the Bahamas for an appearance, after an exhausting press tour for the Hallmark movie, when Art called with an offer from another reality series, *The Real Housewives of Atlanta*. I'd never seen any of *The Real Housewives*, including *Atlanta*, but I knew they were quite the thing—just not my thing. The next day Art sent a follow-up email: The producers understood but they still wanted to talk to me. When we got on the phone several days later, I started the conversation by asking, "Y'all know you called Kim *Fields*, don't you?" Everyone laughed. "Am I being punk'd?" I added.

Besides assuring me that I wasn't being punk'd, they acknowledged being aware the show was out of my wheelhouse. "Then why me?" I asked. They had reasons: The cast was routinely shuffled, and they wanted to add a lighter tone, which they saw me providing. One of the company's top executives called the next day to emphasize their interest. They knew what I stood for, he said. They knew I was not going to engage in the show's trademark confrontations. They were good with that. They did not want to change me. They wanted me as is. They wanted my spirit. They wanted my laughter. And my light.

We also covered the fact that I was involved in projects as a director, producer, entrepreneur, and so on. The show wanted to be informed of those things, in the event they could film them. It appeared, commitment-wise, it was doable with our current obligations. With many other cast members, it seemed like a better fit, logistics-wise, than an entire show revolving around just us.

Later that night, I called Chris and filled him in on the latest. "They also know I'm not a girlfriend type of person," I said. "I told them very clearly that I'm not a hang-out-with-the-girls kind of girl." Chris asked what I thought. "I think they're interested in seeing what this journey might look like," I said. "They know there are a lot of women watching the show who are like me—dedicated to their family, career, and values. They want that voice in their environment."

By the time I returned home, I was intrigued enough to tell Art to tell the producers I was thinking about our conversations. No one was more surprised by this than I was. Chris and I went over the pros and cons. We prayed about it. We sought counsel from family and friends, most of whom told us to pass. Then Chris and I were still and quiet so we could listen to God.

I had to admit, after the initial shock, Chris and I saw more positives than either of us imagined. It was an opportunity for our light to shine on a giant stage in a different arena. *Real Housewives* was a cultural phenomenon, and perhaps we were being given this opportunity to show millions of people what it meant to be dedicated to family, marriage, work, and faith. Last but not least, as I began my fortieth year in the business, I wanted to try new things and challenge myself professionally— go in uncharted career waters.

I knew my fans would wonder why I'd gone into this realm of content. But I felt my reputation could weather any dings, and if people watched, they'd see that I wasn't going to compromise my personal and professional credibility. I was most concerned about the effect on my family, and specifically, my marriage, if I did the show, but Chris dealt with those worries head-on. "Don't worry about us," he said. "We are almost ten years into our marriage. We are strong. We are unbreakable."

That sealed it for me. "Okay," I said, "if we're going to put our toe in the water, it may as well be the ocean; if we're gonna do reality, it might as well be big—and *The Real Housewives of Atlanta* is big."

* * *

From then on, things moved fast. Social media blew up when word got out that I was joining the show. It was September 2015, and fan reaction was all over the map. I learned that *RHOA* fans let you know exactly what they think. To get ready for the style component of this new world, I worked with my stylist, Victoria, on creating a look for the show that was more couture-ish than I wear in my everyday life.

I was supposed to get acquainted with the season eight cast at an event. But as I got out of my car, two producers hurried over and said the network's legal department didn't want me on camera since they hadn't finished my contract.

They introduced me on the show briefly in the second episode. It was a relatively quiet, sane, and respectful point of entry, and I have to say, I was pleasantly surprised the producers chose to show me in a professional light.

I met the rest of the women at an all-cast event. A producer brought a crew to the house to shoot Chris and me getting ready for the party beforehand. They got a window into the real us. I suggested coming up with a safe word for when we were ready to bounce. "How about *discernment?*"

Chris could not even. "That is the worst safety word in the world," he said. "It's not like you can use *discernment* in casual conversation."

* * *

It seemed like my calling it an adventure was a pretty accurate description. There were highs and lows, a couple of fun moments, moments of feeling unsure of where I was going, but still in control . . . And I suppose no adventure is complete without a bit of danger. I came dangerously close to unleashing the Ruthless Assassin Child Star, another nickname from my *Living Single* family for my temper, when folks tried to pull one over on me. We all have that part of us in our back pocket, ready and waiting in the wings (yes, even those of us who try to stayed prayed up . . . Be honest, you know that very prayer is sometimes, "Father, don't let me whoop nobody verbally or otherwise"). I tried to be still but ready for anything. The truth of the matter was, I wasn't going to compromise who I am and what I'm about, how I roll, nor my safety for the sake of a story line. I think most people draw their lines in the sand, not only where they will allow themselves to cross, but also where they will let others cross as it relates to them.

Although, when the police and an ambulance entered at one point, I exited. I tried to be still but ready for anything on this adventure. At times, it was hard to see some of the women interacting the way they did on and for the show.

While we were filming, I still continued my responsibilities as a wife, mom, and career woman. None of those things got put on hold because I was doing the show. Unfortunately, getting into bed at the end of the day did not provide relief nor rest. Have you ever been in an environment where you feel like communicating or existing in that space is like doing mental calisthenics? At work, or school, your neighborhood, or even . . . your church?

As soon as my head hit the pillow, my mind began replaying everything I had said and done in front of the camera. It was an endless scroll of *you should've*'s, *I didn't do*'s, and *next time I'm gonna*'s. It can be tiring dealing with tiresome entities. Yet you have to find the times when you can breathe and laugh . . . because every adventure also needs laughter.

Briefly looking back on the whole season, here's some of what I discerned:

- Being myself, sharing my reality in a quasi-real reality, can be a bizarre vibe.
- Many times as a person with values, home training, or faith we wonder, Why do I have to be the person to take the high road? Why—for just a moment, to put someone in their place—can't I go low when they go low? They can stay there (if they choose to) while I come back up to my regular place. Have you ever felt that way? Why is it that the only time it's acceptable to go down to someone's level is to pick them up? Is the answer as simple as hearing the Lord say, "Because that's what I ask of you, what I expect as your Father, what I require as your creator"? Food for thought . . .

Being true to yourself starts with one word: *True.* Truth . . . opposite of lie. It's not healthy (and to me, there's no reason) to lie to yourself. Be you, do you, boo-boo. As we grow and develop over our lifetimes, I think there are elements that are at our core that are deeply rooted in our soul, so that when we are tried and tested, by people and/or circumstances, that which has taken root grounds us in those moments. Everyone has the ability and power to change whatever they don't like that may have taken root in the negative way, if they choose to. It boils down to choice. What do we choose to take root and why? What do we embrace as our truth, our "true colors" and why? As an actor, we are constantly asking "What's my motivation (to do or say something)?" There were brief moments on the show when I know my face was looking at cast members wondering what in the world motivated them to do or say something. Because it's their job? This is the persona they've carved out for themselves and ID'ing it as their truth?

In my scripted world, we call that acting, making a character you're own. Part of an actor's process is being true to the person you're creating. Remember when I said that process is what drew me in as a little girl at the theater watching *Hello, Dolly!*? Ms. Pearl Bailey was true to herself at the end of every performance of acting as Dolly Levi, when she would talk to the audience from the stage after the curtain call. Once, when she knew I was in the audience, she passed me some cookies from the stage during her time with the audience. That was the performer and friend she truly was.

For much of the filming, I felt like I was in a chess game, constantly ready for and even trying to anticipate the moves of those in front of and behind the camera, while being strategic with my own, while staying a few moves ahead in my mind. Who has the time or desire to communicate and operate like that? Not me. Which is why I opted for being true to myself. My truth, what is deeply rooted in me, is what Mom placed in me: home training, manners, and not selling my soul to the highest bidder. It's what my heroes like Brett Favre and Misty Copeland placed in me, depositing inspiration in my core. My truth is not confrontation but compassion, which enveloped me in my post-9/11 work with the Red Cross at ground zero for the workers in the respite areas.

My deeply rooted strategic thinking efforts don't serve me nearly as well in the "she said-she said" playground, as much as they do in social and cultural arenas, the way Ossie and Ruby, Barack and Michelle, and Bill and Melinda have. I finished my mental calisthenics on rules and safety in the '80s when I navigated my teen years against the backdrop of fame and drugs. So by the time I got into this journey, not being true to myself was never an option. Before I'd made an official statement about doing the show, I quietly cheered so many times when I would see comments on social media when people said they knew I was not gonna let anything or anyone change me.

Yes, I was trying something new, something to stimulate me creatively, professionally, and even a bit personally. While that was attractive to me selfishly speaking, I honestly liked the idea of using my platforms, my voice or celebrity to encourage others to try new things, learn something new, be open...Yet know who you are, so when negativity comes against you, it comes but it doesn't land.

This was a Note to Self I made while filming: When you are strong in who you are and know your truth, it can make those who aren't become a touch unhinged. Hence, be still but ready for anything, wherever you may be being true to yourself.

After five months of filming, the social adventure and its reunion all ended. It was the end of February. I was chairing a Black History Month celebration at Sebastian's school and had to be at chapel at 7:30 a.m. to lead the program. I had two Tuskegee airmen come in and speak to the students. Our theme, which I'd selected, was African American explorers. I'd never compare myself to our Tuskegee heroes, but honestly, I felt like I had done a bit of exploring myself. Doing that brand of TV had been a journey into the unknown, that's for sure. I'd stepped out of my comfort zone and learned new things about myself. I'd tried something new. I hadn't compromised my values in the process. My sense of self and humor had remained intact. I stayed true to myself. Like Chris told me months earlier, "Baby, you have to remember you weren't invited to fit in. You were invited to be yourself."

Ultimately, that was my takeaway and the lesson I had learned and hoped I conveyed to the audience.

#ToeInWaterDidNotDrown
#truetomyself

21

Dancer

While we go through life chronologically, our pasts return randomly and without warning. Memories surface seemingly on their own accord, when needed or necessary. One of my reality cast mates once asked me, "What do you do for yourself? Where's your happy place?" I didn't know what to say. My natural inclination was to take care of people. The postscript on my emails was Proverbs 11:25: "Whoever refreshes others will be refreshed."

I wanted to answer her, but I didn't have an answer for myself. As I continued to think about it, I came to realize that, like so many women, I had missed a crucial step as I focused on a career, added a husband, and had babies by not also making myself a priority—a priority in the deep, emotional, searching, and spiritual way that would enable me to know myself better, to feel better about myself, and, by doing so, to share myself better.

I'd had "me" time back in the late '90s when I came out of my Dark Ages. That was my time to work on me. I'd made myself the priority. I'd known I had to focus on myself in order to move forward in my life. But this was a revelation. It had never occurred to me to make sure I still occasionally made myself a priority, even now—or especially now. If I didn't, I couldn't be at my fullest for anybody else.

So what was I supposed to do? It was December, and Chris and I were spending every free hour finishing the *Holiday Love* show. Then, a few days later, Art called and said *Dancing with the Stars* had invited me on the next season. "What do you think?"

I didn't have to think. As soon as I heard the word *dancing*, it triggered an immediate response. I was in. I was stunned. But I was in.

I marveled at the timing. One show was ending, and the other was getting ready to go into production. Better yet and even more significantly was the way I felt when I thought about doing the show. I'd never danced in my life. I didn't know if I could. And I had to think back to *Battle of the Net-work Stars*, all the way back to the '80s, to remember the last time I'd been in an athletic sort of competition. But all of a sudden my inner voice was shouting at me. *Pay attention!* It desperately wanted me to listen. *This is exactly what you need to do. This is what my cast mate was talking about. This could be your happy place.*

Skeptical at first, I dialogued with myself, asking, *Really?* and hearing a clear response: *Yup, you're going to dance—and you're going to love it.* If the words weren't exactly like that, the feeling I got when I pictured myself doing the show and putting myself out there, in a new, uncertain place, was all positive, and even exciting. I liked the idea of walking to the edge of life's diving board. You have to do that sometimes in order to discover new facets of yourself, and new passions, especially if you want to continue to grow—and I did.

That was why I did *Housewives*. In my fortieth year in

show business, I'd wanted to try something new, and I said the same thing about *Dancing*. But it quickly became obvious to me that *Dancing with the Stars* was more, starting with the connection it would give me to my grandmother, who'd been a professional dancer. I thought about her ripping it up in Harlem's Savoy Ballroom, working with Billy Eckstine, and backing up Pearl Bailey. Perhaps she was the one whispering to me, "You're going to dance—and you're going to love it."

My husband was also a superb dancer—or "a helluva dancer," as my friend Blair Underwood had once said. The show would work with my schedule, meaning I could train in Atlanta. And finally, as everyone knew, doing *Dancing with the Stars* got you in great shape.

So it was like check, check, check—check all the boxes. I was in. I was excited. I was ready to get my dance on.

* * *

But who was going to lead me around the dance floor? Val Chmerkovskiy? Tony Dovolani? Mark Ballas? I had fun anticipating the choice, knowing whoever the producers chose would be right for me; they really don't tell you until the cameras are rolling, and indeed, that's what happened. The show's cameras were at home with me in Atlanta when there was a knock on the front door. I opened it and there stood Sasha Farber, a smile on his face and a bouquet of flowers in his hands. I liked him immediately and even more as we got to know each other.

Born in Russia, he grew up in Australia and was a top competitive dancer starting in his early teens. We had that in common: Both of us had worked since we were kids, and we were still doing what we loved. We discovered other shared traits. We were driven, goal-oriented, and hard workers. We laughed easily. Our birthdays were three days apart. I admitted to being nervous. I wasn't a dancer. Sasha explained that dance was about overcoming obstacles.

Moments later, we moved the living room furniture to the side and Sasha began working with me on basic combinations. He introduced me to the cha-cha. It seemed a little quick, but he said, "You can do this," and there, dressed in my knotted *I Love Lucy*-style work shirt and leggings (I was channeling Lucy auditioning for Ricky at his club) and Chuck Taylors, I said, "Yes, I can."

I wasn't a dancer. But I had no doubt that I would become one.

A week later, my body had second thoughts. On the morning I was supposed to fly to Los Angeles to tape the opening titles and other promotional assets, I woke up feeling dizzy and nauseous. As I soon as I got out of bed, I vomited. "Your body is in shock," my husband said. "Baby, this is the first day you've had off in a week and your body is mad at you. It wants to know what is going on." Sasha said the same thing when I called him in LA to tell him what was happening. "You'll be fine," he said. "You'll adjust."

Just to be sure, Chris took me to the doctor before I got on the plane. She gave me a similar diagnosis. "Drink plenty of water," she said. "Stay hydrated. Get enough rest. Have fun. And good luck." On the plane, between several stretches of sleep, I caught myself smiling at my aching, rebelling body. This was my work ethic kicking into high gear. It was only going to get harder and better, if that makes sense, and if I pushed myself, if I committed to a higher level of excellence, which was my intention, I knew that I would emerge harder and better, too.

By the time I got to Los Angeles, I felt better and eager to see the other celebrity dancers. The field included Marla Maples, meteorologist Ginger Zee, NFL players Antonio Brown and Von Miller, model and activist for the deaf community Nyle DiMarco, former *Full House* and *Fuller House* actress Jodie Sweetin, UFC fighter Paige VanZant, and my dear old friend from Boyz II Men, Wanya Morris, who poked his head into one of my rehearsals and shouted, "You got this!" I offered him similar encouragement. "I'm so proud of you," I said. From the beginning, all of us newbie dancers shared an esprit des corps—if not shared aches and pains. I thought Ginger, Jodie, and Paige looked like the frontrunners, but Sasha didn't want me comparing myself to anyone. "There's no room for those thoughts here," he said. "You have to stay focused on *your* journey."

Wow, where had he been twenty years earlier? *Stay focused on your journey.* Not anyone else's. *Your journey.* Great advice.

The hardest was getting used to Sasha being in my personal space. I'd always been self-conscious, to some degree or another, about my body, and partner dancing is very up close and personal. It's all about the body—moving it, using it, accepting both your gifts and limitations, and in my case, allowing someone else to touch, spin, guide, and lead. It was jarringly intimate. For over a decade the only person (let alone only man) to be in my personal space was Chris.

But this was my issue. It was part of partner dancing, and I adjusted. I had to. During hours and days of rehearsal, my shock turned to surprise and then laughter, and finally acceptance, which was where I had to get in order to compete at this high level. I had to give up some control—actually, a lot of control—to Sasha, and simply let go of those longtime inhibitions and fears about my body. As I told my husband, it was a whole new level of surrender.

I learned, *If it don't kill ya, it makes you stronger, better, wiser, and able to laugh at yourself.*

I bought Sasha a candle and got a matching coffee mug for myself, with the phrase engraved on them: *Life begins where your comfort zone ends.* That was our mantra for our season. Sasha would light the candle every day in rehearsal, and every morning I drank my coffee from that mug. I embraced and clung to that as if it was an additional partner in every number, guiding and empowering me . . . for all six hours of rehearsal six days a week and every time I hit the Ballroom. *Life begins where your comfort zone ends.*

All that said, by the night of the first episode, March 21, 2016, there was not a muscle in my body that had not been twisted, turned, stretched, strained, soothed with Advil, and retrained to dance. Sasha and I were the first couple on the dance floor. I felt good. Amazing, actually. I had gone through so much mentally and physically, and I was ready. I trusted Sasha. He knew what he was doing, and the faith I had in him helped me relax. I also said a little prayer: *Please God, don't let me trip or fall; don't let anything slip out* . . . The extra help couldn't hurt.

As for the dance, Sasha and I performed our routine as rehearsed, but we were so full of adrenaline that it seemed over in a flash. I remembered catching his eye a few times mid-dance and communicating a sense of *Hey, I'm really doing this* and him responding, *I know.* Judge Carrie Ann Inaba called me "fierceness in a tiny package," which left me thrilled and ready for the next one.

Indeed, as week two began, I was super eager to learn new skills and acquire the confidence that came with them. I did my best to come to every rehearsal open-minded, ready to work, and without boundaries. I didn't want anything to inhibit Sasha's creativity for me or us. Dancing was liberating and energizing, and I wanted to go wherever it—and Sasha—would take me. I was willing to try everything. Well, almost everything.

As we prepared a salsa for week two's Latin night, Sasha wanted me to open the number by myself, with a sexy, semi-silhouetted shimmy. As we practiced, I couldn't quite get it right. Each time, he said, "You've got to get into it and shimmy." Finally I heard that one too many times and snapped, "Dude, I don't shimmy. I'm uncomfortable doing that." Chris happened to be watching the rehearsal and he encouraged me to listen to Sasha. "I think you can shimmy," he said. "You just have to be less inhibited."

I agreed to try, but it was easier said than done. Sasha had me pin two tassels to my shirt—right on my chest, like a stripper! "We're not moving on until those tassels move," he said. I had an idea of what he wanted me to do but no knowledge of how to do it. Frustrated, I stopped myself on the verge of tears and said to myself, *Oh man, this chick can't show up right now. Just push through it. Own it.*

We were dancing to Gloria Estefan's hit "Conga." She was a hero of mine, and Sasha arranged for a surprise Skype session with her between rehearsals. I screamed when I saw it was Gloria live on the computer. "I'm rooting for you," she said. We invited her to watch us run through our dance, and afterward she was full of encouragement. "You're absolutely fabulous and beautiful," she said. "You're going to get amazing points on this because you're awesome."

Talk about being in a happy place. I'd opened myself to risk, and look where it had taken me. Even better, we made it, sailing through the round!

Next, we did the foxtrot to the *Facts of Life* theme song, which was the show's choice, not mine. I wanted to be taken more seriously. My sister watched one of the rehearsals and blew me away by saying that she could see a new level of confidence in me. I felt it, too. This is why I'd said yes to the show.

As the season progressed, the dances got longer. Sasha added choreography and warned me to pace myself. That was funny. I didn't know how to pace myself in anything, and frankly, I didn't care. As far as I was concerned, *Dancing* was about pushing myself to new limits, not pacing myself. I wasn't about to slow down. I was in the best shape of my life.

I was drinking healthy smoothies and eating fresh fruits and vegetables during the day, and for dinner, I ate chicken. The weight melted off me, and I saw a toned dancer's body in its place.

Sasha made me text him photos of myself at each meal to prove that I was eating enough, and my wonderful husband sent reminders to me to hydrate. I received calls, emails, and texts from friends, rooting for me. My mom and sister provided invaluable support. Chris was amazing. My boys finished every call saying, "Good night, Mommy. Good luck. You're the best dancer in the world."

Hardly. But I went to sleep satisfied that I was working hard to become the best dancer I could be, and I woke up full of energy, ready to hit the studio. I was focused, and fulfilled. I'd crossed numerous personal barriers—vulnerability, embarrassment, and uncertainty—and tapped into beauty, grace, joy, confidence, and a sense that I could do anything I set my mind and body to.

* * *

During a rehearsal for week four, Disney Night, I was jumping on the balls of my feet for our quickstep and felt a pull. Sasha knew right away that I'd injured the tendons around my Achilles. The show sent me to a doctor who checked for ankle sprains and hairline fractures. As I waited for the MRI, Sasha had me practicing moves in the lobby of the doctor's office. I brushed off the doctor's recommendation to lay off rehearsals. "I've had two children," I said. "This little thing ain't nothin'."

Who doesn't have aches and pains? Hadn't Sasha said dancing was overcoming obstacles? I felt great and was thriving in what I realized was my happy place. I also thrived on the camaraderie with the others. Early on, Ginger Zee and I laughed at how awful all of us gals looked on camera in the rehearsals, sweaty and messy, like we'd been tossed all over the place, which we had! I loved that she was the scrappy, nerdy kid who liked science.

For Disney Night, Chris and Sebastian flew into town (Quincy was always with me and hung at my mom's while I worked) and cheered on Sasha and me as we made it through another round. I was in a zone with Sasha as we got to Switch Up Week, which threw me, as it's supposed to. I was paired with South African pro Latin and Ballroom dancer, Keo Motsepe, who'd surprised me in the rehearsal studio. I'd expected to be partnered with Mark Ballas or Val Chmerkovskiy. I didn't think they'd put two black people together. Keo was also so much taller than me. Much.

We went through a quick, frank getting-to-know-each-other process as he ushered me through the waltz. During one rehearsal, we were dancing close and I felt something hard near his pocket. "Are you kidding me?" I exclaimed. He stopped, stepped back, and reached into his pocket, laughing and embarrassed. "No, no, no, it's my microphone pack!" My mother and Aunt Pat both cried when they saw us in costume on the show; they said I looked and moved so much like my grandmother. I was overjoyed in my soul.

I was glad to have Sasha back the next week and we worked super hard on our jive to the great song from *Hairspray*, "You Can't Stop the Beat." We got a great score from the judges and crucial support from fans, and it sent me into the following week thinking we had a chance to make it to the finals. But there were still several rounds before then, starting with Icons Week. Sasha and I were assigned the Jackson 5's "ABC." Great song, but it was challenging for Sasha to create a samba to the bubblegum classic. We spiced it up with backup dancers. We even had a cool black light with neon paint effect, and Sasha's choreography was really fantastic.

* * *

Until we were eliminated, I had no sense we'd be going home. I was stunned and devastated. The snot cry that came out of me was real. I kept thinking, *Be gracious. Keep it together, Kimmy. Be gracious.* But inside, I could hear myself screaming, wanting to get real with Tom Bergeron, the audience in the ballroom, and all those watching at home. "Tom, you know this ain't right. I'm not supposed to get voted off right now. I ain't leaving this mutha! This is some mistake and my black self ain't goin' nowhere!!!!!!!!!!!!"

Can you imagine what that would've been like?

But that's the way I felt—robbed. I cried my way back to my trailer, hearing whispers of supportive words from those around me. My sister helped me through the shock and disappointment. As was the routine for the eliminated team, Sasha and I had to appear live on *Good Morning America* from New York the next morning, so I hurried to my apartment, threw a change of clothes into a bag, and raced to the airport. On the way, I called Chris, who apologized for being unable to console me because he had to console Sebastian, who'd snuck out of his bedroom, watched me get eliminated, and was having his own hard time.

At the airport, I was met by a woman from Delta airlines who handed me a box of See's candy. "I was watching," she said. "I can't believe you're here right now." Neither could I. Then, after a security delay, I missed my flight. Sasha, who was already on the plane, texted me with a heart symbol: "I am so proud of you." After I caught a later flight, we reconvened at the *Good Morning America* studio, where Robin Roberts gave me a hug to end all hugs, one of those all-enveloping body wraps where she let her heart beat into mine in a way that said, *You're going to be okay, l'il sis.*

And I was.

I was better than okay.

* * *

And that was the point. I was okay before *Dancing with the Stars,* but I was even better afterward. Yes, part of the reason I went on the show was to continue my professional narrative, to try projects and genres I hadn't done. But it was also something I did for myself, something that nourished me deep down as a human being. It was, as I had hoped, my new happy place. Though I returned home the day after *Good Morning America* and went back to my husband and children, packing lunches, driving in school carpools, reading scripts, and developing projects, my life was different. At age forty-seven, I proved it is never too late to learn something new, acquire a new passion, and find your happy place.

Like dancing, I couldn't have cha-cha-cha'ed or waltzed without help from other people. Isn't that what we learn about life? It's a group effort. Family and friends all pitched in. Not only did I have to let them, but I was also reminded of why, as I've mentioned before, the postscript on my emails is Proverbs 11:25: "Whoever refreshes others will be refreshed." The connection between us only deepens when we allow someone to lend a hand and make our journey a little easier. As Blair said to me decades ago, "It's okay to ask for help. When you do, you allow others to bless you. When you don't, they can't. Don't be a blessing blocker."

Finally, people of faith talk about surrendering to God's will. I certainly have said my fair share about it. But do we really know how to let go? If I didn't know before, I know now what it is like to completely let go and trust in the Lord. In order to dance, I had to surrender to my discomfort with my body. I had to surrender to my teacher. I had to surrender to a blind faith that Sasha would teach me the steps and that the steps would come to me if I learned them, practiced them, and took them to heart. I had to surrender life—and live it. And I had to surrender to love—knowing that my family would still love me when I got back and that I would love myself even more for taking this risk and ultimately that I would be able to love all of them even more for having opened myself up to this great, grand adventure.

Oh, there's one more thing. I learned that I could dance.

And I love to dance.

Oh God, I love to dance—and plan to keep on dancing.

Epilogue

In the meantime, here I am. It's been a year since that last night on *Dancing with the Stars* and several months since I wrote the first sentence of this book. At this moment, I'm heading to Atlanta from Savannah, on my way home from the set of a wonderful new British TV comedy I'm starring in for Sky 1 called *Living the Dream*. This past week I enjoyed several good days where I nailed my work and one frustrating day where things were just a little off. That's the way it goes for all of us, right?

I remember a song whose lyrics went, "You take the good, you take the bad, you take them both and there you have . . ."

You know how that one goes, I think.

Anyway, here in my car, I am reflecting on where and why I began this book, and where I am at this moment, and I have to reiterate what I said at the outset—that my life has been a journey along a road like the one I'm on now. Sometimes I have driven on one side, sometimes I have driven on the other side, and then there are those times when I have ridden the line down the middle. What I've come to terms with is that as long as I'm moving forward in one direction, I'm winning at least half the battle.

Speaking of *Battle*, how much did I love competing in the reboot of *Battle of the Network Stars*? Yes, somewhere in my soul with every event, I hoped I'd make Mark Harmon and Michael J. Fox proud.

Here's what I also know: The sum of my experiences—all the laughs and the tears, the love and the heartbreak, the disappointments and the joys, and all the chances I've taken, and survived—are what enables me to know that I can handle whatever the future brings. Like everyone, I wish some things had been easier. But writing this book has reminded me that I've been much more resilient than I might have felt at the time I was going through stuff. Aren't we all?

I see the way decisions and events have shaped me. I see the myriad ways other people have helped and inspired me along the way. I see my village and cherish the friendship, love, and faith we've shared with each other. I see that I probably worried more than I needed to. I see that God was always with me, ready to help and guide me, especially when I felt confused, frustrated, and alone. I see that I am not always in control, not the way I often think. I see a deeper level of surrender since *Dancing with the Stars*, one where I can truly let go and let God and trust Him to lead. Working in the movie *A Question of Faith* recently confirmed so much of this again, as I portrayed a woman dealing with these very issues when her family and world is turned upside down.

I see that I wouldn't change a thing I've been through on the chance it would alter where I am right now, which is loving and loved, and mostly happy, sometimes harried, incredibly grateful, and always trying to keep it real.

Chris and I have lived in Atlanta for nearly a decade now, with our place in Harlem still in our grasp. I didn't expect to plant roots and raise my children here, but I couldn't have planned anything over the past forty-eight years, and as you've come to see in this book, I didn't. And when I did try to plan, well, we know what happened then. In the meantime, He has had me act and direct and create music and perform poetry. He has taken me from Harlem to Hollywood and beyond. He has blessed me with life and the gift to live it with passion and love. He has surrounded me with wonderful family and friends.

Chris and I talk about this all the time, the real gifts of life as opposed to those we mistakenly believe are important. I realize there's an enormous amount of irony in the fact that the Gypsy life we live is exactly the type of life I always tried to avoid. I attribute it to God's divine humor. Every time I made plans, He said, "Guess what, Boo-Boo?" and then showed me who's really in the driver's seat.

If I had the safety net I always thought I wanted, I wonder if I would look for Him less. Would I be less tuned to His voice?

All I know is that I love where I am now with my husband, my family, and my faith.

My faith is the driving force in my life, and I feel that if I follow Him forward, as our friend Israel Houghton so beautifully put it in his song "Moving Forward": "I'm not going back, moving ahead . . . " I will continue to grow and move forward and ultimately get where I'm supposed to be. I will be all right. If you're like me, you believe that none of us are alone. We're connected directly and indirectly, in ways we don't even know, and also in that miraculous way we all are well aware of and best to remember—through our capacity to give and receive love. That's our lifeline. That's His message. That's our connection with each other. That's what I had in mind at the beginning of this book when I said that this story was not just my journey, but our journey together.

At some point every day, no matter what's happened, something reminds me of how much life is worth living. It might be a smile, something I came across on the Internet, a phone call, a memory, or a flash of beauty I glimpse out the window. Through losses I've come to understand the value.

*　*　*

Travel update: Only forty miles more until I'm home and get to climb into my own bed. I am also looking forward to my birthday, which is two days from now. Chris and I will drive back to Savannah for the weekend. We'll take Sebastian and Quincy, too. We all will hang out at my favorite spot on the river, have a nice family dinner, and celebrate together. The boys will help me blow out my birthday candles. They'll ask how old I am, and when I say I'm forty-eight, they'll say, "Wow, that's old."

The truth is, it's not old. It's exciting. It's great. I'm thrilled to be here and I'll tell my mom that when we talk, when I thank her as I do every birthday for having me. I'm eager to watch my children grow up and am hopeful about their lives. I'm looking forward to my marriage continuing to fulfill, challenge, and surprise me. As for work, I plan to go on forever. Actors only get better with age. The more you live, the more you bring to a role. As you can see, I am positive, ambitious, and full of hope and dreams, as I am about life itself, and I hope that came across in this book.

We all have the ability to sharpen each other, inspire each other, to be stronger and better without being disrespectful, without being hateful, without being self-righteous. We have the ability to love ourselves and each other, and that should be our goal. We're on this journey together. There are blessings all around us. Even more, we all have the amazing ability to *be* the blessing.

Life itself is a blessing. It has been for me.

*　*　*

Thank you for being on this road with me. Now, let's keep going.

Love,
Kim

Acknowledgments

It takes a village to raise a celebrity. I have a few mini-villages within my village that deserve acknowledgment, deep gratitude, and praise. Not only would this book not have gotten done, but this life would not be nearly as blessed without them...

Team Kim Village:

Art Rutter, Valerie Enloe, Paul Wright III, Michelle Grant, Kymberlee Norsworthy, Julia McCrank, and Ki Cottrell

Publishing Village:

Dan Strone, Keren Baltzer (you're amazing, thank you for your role in this process and doing it so beautifully), Nicci Jordan Hubert (thank you for your editing gifts and talents!), Grace Johnson, Patsy Jones, and all of Hachette Book Group

Artists Village:

Erykah Badu; Lalah Hathaway; Maxwell; Yolanda Adams; Malcolm-Jamal Warner; Blair Underwood; Fred Hammond; Israel Houghton; Kels and Hali Johnson; Vincent and Ebony Powell; Yvette Nicole Brown; Najee; Fareed; literary inspirations Pat Conroy, Judy Blume, Langston Hughes, and Brad

Thor; Holiday Love family and friends; Curtis King; and The Dee-Davis families

Life Village:

The Hurds; The Morgans; The Jacksons; The Loopers; The Blakes; The Shaltos; The Bells; The Mellinis; Victoria Shaffer; Paula Monette; Erica Strong; The Potts; Joyer; Brianna Robinson; The Bazemores; Carol Kim; Bishop Charles Blake and the Blake Family; The Gross and Perkins Families; every sitter; Lower School's JB, BW, family and friends; every Glam Squad; every media outlet; every fan

My Voice Village of One:

Todd Gold. What can I possibly say? Your hard work, dedication, gifts, and talents as a writer and biographer are extraordinary. I could not have done this without you. This time of reflection, discovery, revelations, and examination—laced with laughs and tears—has been a glorious journey to be treasured forever. Thank you. Thank you.

If a name is not listed it does not mean your spirit is not strong in my heart or that your presence is not strong in my village...it simply means I did not have enough coffee while writing this.

About the Author

KIM FIELDS had her first job at age seven on the Mrs. Butterworth syrup commercial. She's spent forty years in the public eye. There were nine years as Dorothy "Tootie" Ramsey on the classic sitcom *The Facts of Life*, five more in her twenties co-starring on the seminal coming-of-age show *Living Single*, and most recently she appeared as herself on *Real Housewives of Atlanta* and *Dancing with the Stars*. Behind the camera, she directed episodes of *Kenan & Kel*, *Tyler Perry's Meet the Browns* and *House of Payne*, and BET's *Let's Stay Together*. Between gigs her life has included theater, spoken word, music, and speaking engagements. She is a dedicated wife and proud mom of two boys.